CHILDREN'S ENCYCLOPEDIA
DINOSAURS
AND PREHISTORIC LIFE

CHILDREN'S ENCYCLOPEDIA
DINOSAURS
AND PREHISTORIC LIFE

Miles
Kelly

First published in 2013 by Miles Kelly Publishing Ltd
Harding's Barn, Bardfield End Green, Thaxted, Essex, CM6 3PX, UK

Copyright © Miles Kelly Publishing Ltd 2013

2 4 6 8 10 9 7 5 3 1

Publishing Director Belinda Gallagher
Creative Director Jo Cowan
Cover Designer Simon Lee
Designers Jo Cowan, Rob Hale, Venita Kidwai,
Simon Lee, Sophie Pelham, Andrea Slane
Indexer Eleanor Holme
Image Manager Liberty Newton
Production Manager Elizabeth Collins
Reprographics Stephan Davis, Jenni Hunt, Thom Allaway
Contributors Rupert Matthews, Steve Parker

ISBN 978-1-78209-110-3

Printed in China

British Library Cataloguing-in-Publication Data
A catalogue record for this book is available from the British Library

Made with paper from a sustainable forest

www.mileskelly.net
info@mileskelly.net

www.factsforprojects.com

CONTENTS

PREHISTORIC LIFE 8–49

DINOSAURS 50–91

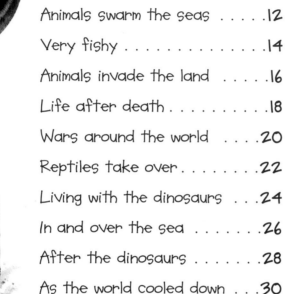

T REX

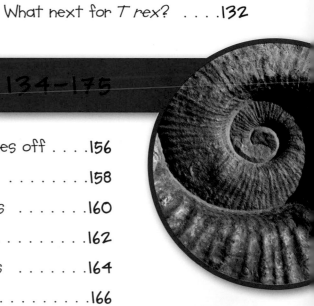

FOSSILS

EXTINCT

PREHISTORIC LIFE

1 The Earth was once covered by huge sheets of ice. This happened several times during Earth's history and we call these frozen times ice ages. However, the ice ages are a tiny part of prehistory. Before then, the world was warm and lakes and seas covered the land. Even earlier than this, there was little rain for thousands of years, and the land was covered in deserts. Over millions of years weather and conditions changed. Living things changed too, in order to survive. This change is called 'evolution'.

Woolly rhinoceros

Cave lion

▼ A scene from the last ice age, about 10,000 years ago. Animals grew thick fur coats to protect themselves from the cold. Many animals, such as woolly mammoths, survived on plants such as mosses. Others, such as cave lions, were fierce hunters, needing meat to survive.

Aurochs

Woolly mammoth

Megaloceros

Life begins

2 **Life began a very, very long time ago.** We know this from the remains of prehistoric life forms that died and were buried. Over millions of years, their remains turned into shapes in rocks, called fossils. The first fossils are over 3000 million years old. They are tiny 'blobs' called bacteria – living things that still survive today.

3 **The first plants were seaweeds, which appeared about 1000 million years ago.** Unlike bacteria and blue-green algae, which each had just one living cell, these plants had thousands of cells. Some seaweeds were many metres long. They were called algae – the same name that scientists use today.

4 **By about 800 million years ago, some plants were starting to grow on land.** They were mixed with other living things called moulds, or fungi. Together, the algae (plants) and fungi formed flat green-and-yellow crusts that crept over rocks and soaked up rain. They were called lichens. These still grow on rocks and trees today.

▼ Fossils of *Anomalocaris* have been found in Canada. It had a circular mouth and finlike body parts. Its body was covered by a shell.

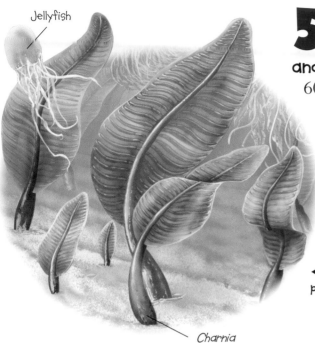

Jellyfish

Charnia

5 The first animals lived in the sea – and they were as soft as jelly! Over 600 million years ago, some of the first animals were jellyfish, floating in the water. On the seabed lived groups of soft, feathery-looking creatures called *Charnia*. This animal was an early type of coral. Animals need to take in food by eating other living things. *Charnia* caught tiny plants in its 'feathers'.

◀ *Charnia* looked like a prehistoric plant, but it was actually an animal!

6 One of the first hunting animals was *Anomalocaris*. It lived 520 million years ago, swimming through the sea in search of prey. It caught smaller creatures in its pincers, then pushed them into its mouth. *Anomalocaris* was a cousin of crabs and insects. It was one of the biggest hunting animals of its time, even though it was just 60 centimetres in length

▲ The *Cooksonia* plant had forked stems that carried water. The earliest examples have been found in Ireland.

7 By 400 million years ago, plants on land were growing taller. They had stiff stems that held them upright and carried water to their topmost parts. An early upright plant was *Cooksonia*. Even though it was the tallest thing on land, it was only 5 centimetres high – barely the size of your thumb!

Animals swarm the seas

8 **Some of the first common animals were worms.** However, they were not earthworms in soil. At the time there was no soil and the land was bare. These worms lived in the sea. They burrowed in mud for plants and animals to eat.

◀ *Ottoia* was a sea worm that fed by filtering tiny food particles from the sea.

▼ Trilobites moved quickly across the seabed. Some could roll up into a ball like woodlice do today. This was a means of protection.

9 **The next animals to become common were trilobites.** They first lived about 550 million years ago in the sea. Trilobites crawled along the seabed eating tiny bits of food they found. Their name means 'three lobes' (parts). A trilobite had two grooves along its back, from head to tail, so its body had three main parts – left, middle and centre.

▼ *Pterygotus* was a fierce hunter, with large eyes and long claws.

10 **Trilobites were some of the first animals with legs that bent at the joints.** Animals with jointed legs are called arthropods. They have been the most common creatures for millions of years, including trilobites long ago, and later on, crabs, spiders and insects. Like other arthropods, trilobites had a tough, outer shell for protection.

11 **Some of the first hunters were sea scorpions – some were as big as lions!** *Pterygotus* was 2 metres long. It swished its tail to chase prey through water, which it tore apart with its huge claws. Sea scorpions lived 500 to 250 million years ago. Unlike modern scorpions, they had no sting in their tails.

12 For millions of years the seabed was covered with the curly shells of ammonites. Some of these shells were as small as your fingernail, others were bigger than dinner plates. Ammonites were successful creatures and thousands of kinds survived for millions of years. Each ammonite had big eyes to see prey and long tentacles (arms) to catch it with. Ammonites died out at the same time as the dinosaurs, around 65 million years ago.

▲ This rock contains an ammonite fossil. The shell would have protected the soft-bodied creature inside.

◄ *Pikaia* looked a little bit like an eel with fins.

13 Among the worms, trilobites and ammonites was a small creature that had a very special body part — the beginnings of a backbone. It was called *Pikaia* and lived about 530 million years ago. Gradually, more animals with backbones, called vertebrates, evolved from it. Today, vertebrates rule much of the world — they are fish, reptiles, birds and mammals.

QUIZ

1. Did sea scorpions have stings in their tails?
2. What does the name 'trilobite' mean?
3. What kind of animal was *Ottoia*?
4. When did ammonites die out?
5. What was special about *Pikaia*?

Answers:
1. No 2. Three lobes, or parts 3. A worm 4. 65 million years ago 5. It had an early type of backbone

Very fishy

14 The first fish could not bite — they were suckers! About 500 million years ago, new animals appeared in the sea — the first fish. They had no jaws or teeth and probably sucked in worms and small pieces of food from the mud.

▲ *Hemicyclaspis* was an early jawless fish. It had eyes on top of its head and probably lived on the seabed. This way it could keep a look out for predators above.

15 Some early fish wore suits of armour! They had hard, curved plates of bone all over their bodies for protection. These fish were called placoderms and most were fierce hunters. Some had huge jaws with sharp sheets of bone for slicing up prey.

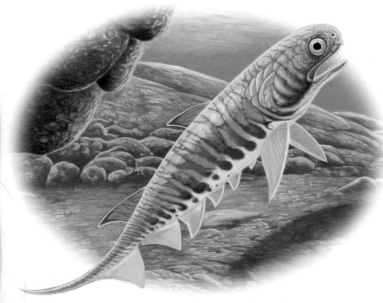

16 Spiny sharks had spines, but they were not really sharks. These fish were similar in shape to today's sharks, but they lived in rivers and lakes, not the sea, about 430 million years ago. *Climatius* was a spiny shark that looked fierce, but it was only as big as your finger!

◄ The fins on the back of *Climatius* were supported by needle-sharp spines. These helped to protect it from attacks by squid or other fish.

17
The first really big hunting fish was bigger than today's great white shark! *Dunkleosteus* grew to almost 10 metres in length and swam in the oceans 360 million years ago. It sliced up prey, such as other fish, using its huge teeth made of narrow blades of bone, each one as big as this book.

18
Some early fish started to 'walk' out of water. Types of fish called lobefins appeared 390 million years ago. Their side fins each had a 'stump' at the base made of muscle. If the water in their pool dried up, lobefins could use their fins like stubby legs to waddle over land to another pool. *Eusthenopteron* was a lobefin fish about one metre long. Over millions of years, some lobefins evolved into four-legged animals called tetrapods.

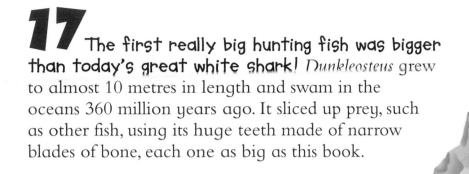

VERY FISHY!
You will need:
waxed card (like the kind used to make milk cartons) crayons scissors piece of soap

Place the piece of waxed card face down. Fold the card up at the edges. Draw a fish on the card. Cut a small notch in the rear of the card and wedge the piece of soap in it. Put the 'fish' in a bath of cold water and watch it swim away.

▼ *Eusthenopteron* could clamber about on dry land when moving from one stretch of water to another.

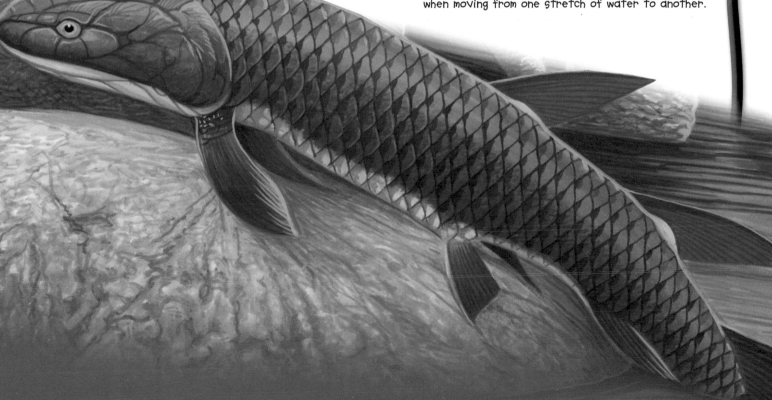

Animals invade the land

19 The first land animals lived about 450 million years ago. These early creatures, which came from the sea, were arthropods – creatures with hard outer body casings and jointed legs. They included prehistoric insects, spiders and millipedes. *Arthropleura* was a millipede – it was 2 metres in length!

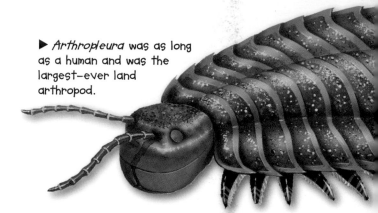

▶ *Arthropleura* was as long as a human and was the largest-ever land arthropod.

20 Some amphibians were fierce hunters. *Gerrothorax* was about one metre long and spent most of its time at the bottom of ponds or streams. Its eyes pointed upward, to see fish swimming past, just above. *Gerrothorax* would then jump up to grab the fish in its wide jaws.

21 The first four-legged animal had eight toes on each front foot! *Acanthostega* used its toes to grip water plants as it swam. It lived about 380 million years ago and was one metre long. Creatures like it soon began to walk on land, too. They were called tetrapods, which means 'four legs'. They were a big advance in evolution – the first land animals with backbones.

◀ *Acanthostega* probably spent most of its time in water. It had gills for breathing underwater as well as lungs for breathing air.

22 Soon four-legged animals called amphibians were racing across the land. Amphibians were the first backboned animals to move fast out of the water. *Aphaneramma* had long legs and could run quickly. However, prehistoric amphibians, like those of today such as frogs and newts, had to return to the water to lay their eggs.

23 Fins became legs for walking on land, and tails changed, too. As the fins of lobefin fish evolved into legs, their tails became longer and more muscular. *Ichthyostega* had a long tail with a fin along its upper side. This tail design was good for swimming in water, and also helpful when wriggling across a swamp.

24 Some amphibians grew as big as crocodiles! *Eogyrinus* was almost 5 metres long and had strong jaws and teeth, like a crocodile. However, it lived about 300 million years ago, long before any crocodiles appeared. Although *Eogyrinus* could walk on dry land, it spent most of its time in streams and swamps.

◀ *Ichthyostega* had short legs, so it could probably only move slowly on land.

Life after death

25 **There were times in prehistory when almost everything died out.** These times are called mass extinctions. Just a few types of plants and animals survive, which can then change, or evolve, into new kinds. A mass extinction about 290 million years ago allowed a fairly new group of animals to spread fast – the reptiles.

26 **Reptiles' skin and eggs helped them to survive.** Unlike an amphibian's, a reptile's scaly skin was waterproof. Also, the jelly-like eggs of amphibians had to be laid in water, while a reptile's eggs had tough shells for surviving on land. Around 280 million years ago, reptiles such as 1.5-metre-long *Varanosaurus* were spreading to dry areas where amphibians could not survive.

EDIBLE REPTILES

You will need:
100 grams dried milk   100 grams smooth peanut butter   2 tablespoons honey   currants   food colouring

Mix the dried milk, peanut butter and honey in a bowl. Mould this paste into reptile shapes. Decorate with currants for eyes and add food colouring for bright skin patterns. Then cause a mass extinction – eat them!

▲ *Varanosaurus* lived in what is now Texas, USA, and may have hunted fish in swamps.

▶ *Hylonomus* lived in forests in what is now Canada. It hunted insects, spiders and millipedes.

27 **The first reptile looked like a lizard.** However *Hylonomus* belonged to a different reptile group to lizards. It lived like a lizard, chasing prey on the ground and in trees. It lived 345 million years ago.

28 **Some reptiles started to avoid bad weather by sleeping underground.** *Diictodon* lived about 260 million years ago and used its large teeth to chop up tough plant food. It may have dug holes to shelter from the heat, cold and rain.

▼ *Diictodon* had strong legs and sharp claws for burrowing.

29 Some amphibians fought back against the reptiles. *Mastodonsaurus* was a big, strong amphibian, 2 metres long, with sharp teeth. It hunted fish, other amphibians, and small reptiles. It lived at a time when reptiles were spreading even faster, about 250 to 203 million years ago. But most other big amphibians did not survive the reptiles.

▼ The nostrils and eyes of *Mastodonsaurus* were on top of its head so that it could breathe and look around whilst hiding underwater.

30 Other amphibians managed to survive the reptile takeover, too. They were mainly small and hid in water or swamps. One was *Branchiosaurus*, which was about 12 centimetres long and hunted small fish in ponds.

▲ *Lystrosaurus* lived in Antarctica when it was a land of lush, tropical plant life. Today it is a frozen continent, covered by thick ice.

31 Reptiles showed how the world's lands moved about. *Lystrosaurus* lived about 200 million years ago and its fossils come from Europe, Asia, Africa and Antarctica. This reptile could not swim, so all of these landmasses, or continents, must have been joined together at one time. Over millions of years, they drifted apart to form today's positions.

▼ As well as sharp teeth, *Moschops* had very strong skull bones, so it may have head-butted rivals in fights.

32 Some plant-eating reptiles had very sharp teeth. *Moschops* was as big as a rhino and lived in southern Africa about 270 million years ago. Its teeth were long and straight, and ended with a sharp edge like a chisel. *Moschops* could easily bite tough leaves and twigs off bushes.

Reptiles take over

33 Reptiles don't like to be too hot, or too cold. Otherwise they may overheat, or be too cold to move. Most reptiles bask in sunshine to get warm, then stay in the shade. *Dimetrodon* was a fierce reptile. It had a large 'sail' of skin on its back to soak up heat from the sun.

▲ The name *Dimetrodon* means 'two-types-of-teeth'. It was given this name as it had stabbing teeth and slicing teeth. It measured 3 metres in length.

34 The first crocodiles hated water! An early type of crocodile, *Protosuchus*, stayed on land. It lived in North America about 190 million years ago. It was one metre long and could run across dry land when hunting, using its long legs.

▶ *Protosuchus* had very powerful jaw muscles to snap its teeth shut on prey.

▶ *Chasmatosaurus* had teeth on the roof of its mouth as well as in its jaws.

35 **Some reptiles moved by using their tails.** Many early reptiles had long, strong tails. They probably lived in water and swished their tails to push themselves along. *Chasmatosaurus* was 2 metres long and probably hunted for fish. It looked like a crocodile but was more closely related to the dinosaurs.

36 **Some reptiles began to look very much like mammals.** *Cynognathus* was as big as a large dog, and instead of scaly skin it had fur. It belonged to a group of reptiles called therapsids. Around 220 million years ago, some types of small therapsids were evolving into the first mammals.

◀ The jaws of *Cynognathus* were so powerful they could bite through bone. Its name means 'dog jaw'.

Living with the dinosaurs

37 Some reptiles were as big and fierce as dinosaurs – but they lived in the sea. One of these was *Mosasaurus*. It grew up to 10 metres in length and may have weighed 10 tonnes, far bigger than today's great white shark.

38 One sea reptile had teeth the size of saucers! The huge, round, flat teeth of *Placodus* were more than 10 centimetres across. It used them to crush shellfish and sea urchins. *Placodus* was about 2 metres long and lived at the same time as the first dinosaurs, around 230 million years ago.

I DON'T BELIEVE IT!
Fossils of *Mosasaurus* were found in the same place over 200 years apart! The first was found in a quarry in the Netherlands in 1780. The second was found in the same place in 1998.

▼ *Mosasaurus* was a huge sea reptile. It had razor-sharp teeth and could swim with speed to catch its prey.

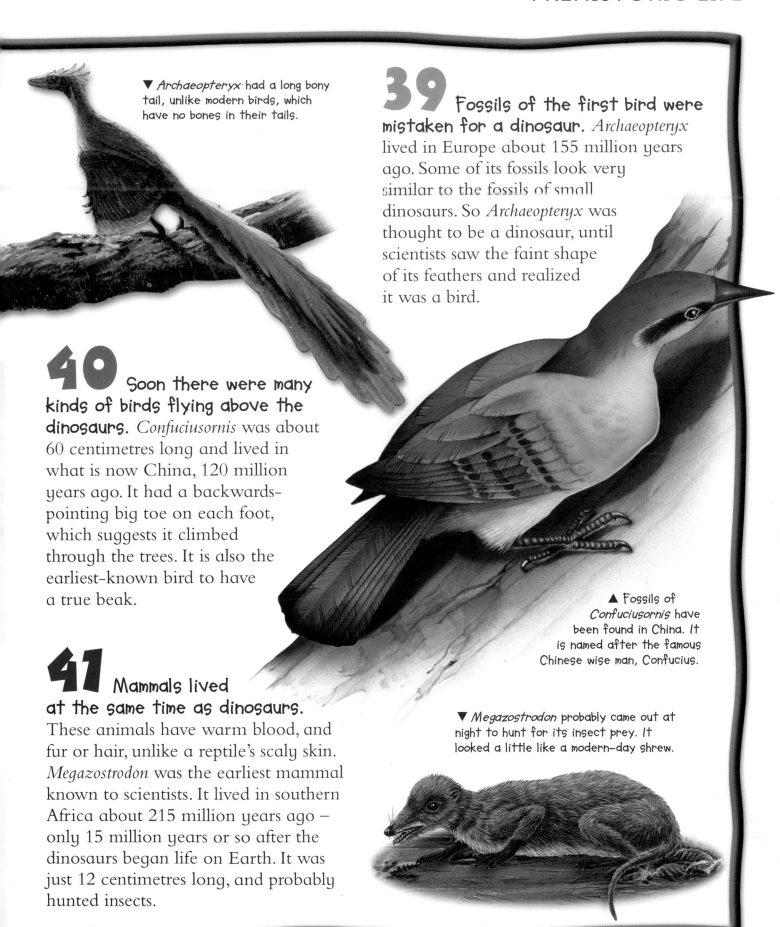

▼ *Archaeopteryx* had a long bony tail, unlike modern birds, which have no bones in their tails.

39 Fossils of the first bird were mistaken for a dinosaur. *Archaeopteryx* lived in Europe about 155 million years ago. Some of its fossils look very similar to the fossils of small dinosaurs. So *Archaeopteryx* was thought to be a dinosaur, until scientists saw the faint shape of its feathers and realized it was a bird.

40 Soon there were many kinds of birds flying above the dinosaurs. *Confuciusornis* was about 60 centimetres long and lived in what is now China, 120 million years ago. It had a backwards-pointing big toe on each foot, which suggests it climbed through the trees. It is also the earliest-known bird to have a true beak.

▲ Fossils of *Confuciusornis* have been found in China. It is named after the famous Chinese wise man, Confucius.

41 Mammals lived at the same time as dinosaurs. These animals have warm blood, and fur or hair, unlike a reptile's scaly skin. *Megazostrodon* was the earliest mammal known to scientists. It lived in southern Africa about 215 million years ago – only 15 million years or so after the dinosaurs began life on Earth. It was just 12 centimetres long, and probably hunted insects.

▼ *Megazostrodon* probably came out at night to hunt for its insect prey. It looked a little like a modern-day shrew.

In and over the sea

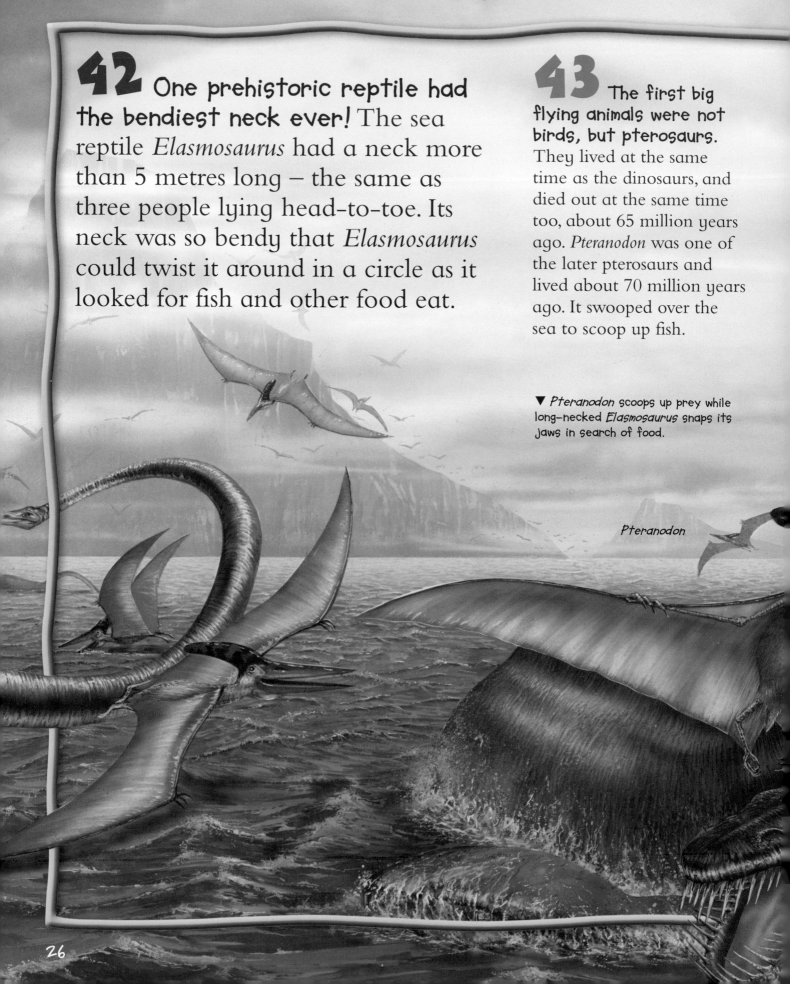

42 One prehistoric reptile had the bendiest neck ever! The sea reptile *Elasmosaurus* had a neck more than 5 metres long – the same as three people lying head-to-toe. Its neck was so bendy that *Elasmosaurus* could twist it around in a circle as it looked for fish and other food eat.

43 The first big flying animals were not birds, but pterosaurs. They lived at the same time as the dinosaurs, and died out at the same time too, about 65 million years ago. *Pteranodon* was one of the later pterosaurs and lived about 70 million years ago. It swooped over the sea to scoop up fish.

▼ *Pteranodon* scoops up prey while long-necked *Elasmosaurus* snaps its jaws in search of food.

Pteranodon

44 **The largest flying animal of all time was as big as a plane!** With wings measuring up to 14 metres from tip to tip, the pterosaur *Quetzalcoatlus* was twice as big as any flying bird. It may have lived like a vulture, soaring high in the sky, and then landing to peck at a dead body of a dinosaur.

45 **Some fossils of sea creatures are found thousands of kilometres from the sea.** Around 100 to 70 million years ago, much of what is now North America was flooded. The shallow waters teemed with all kinds of fish, reptiles and other creatures. Today their fossils are found on dry land.

Elasmosaurus

After the dinosaurs

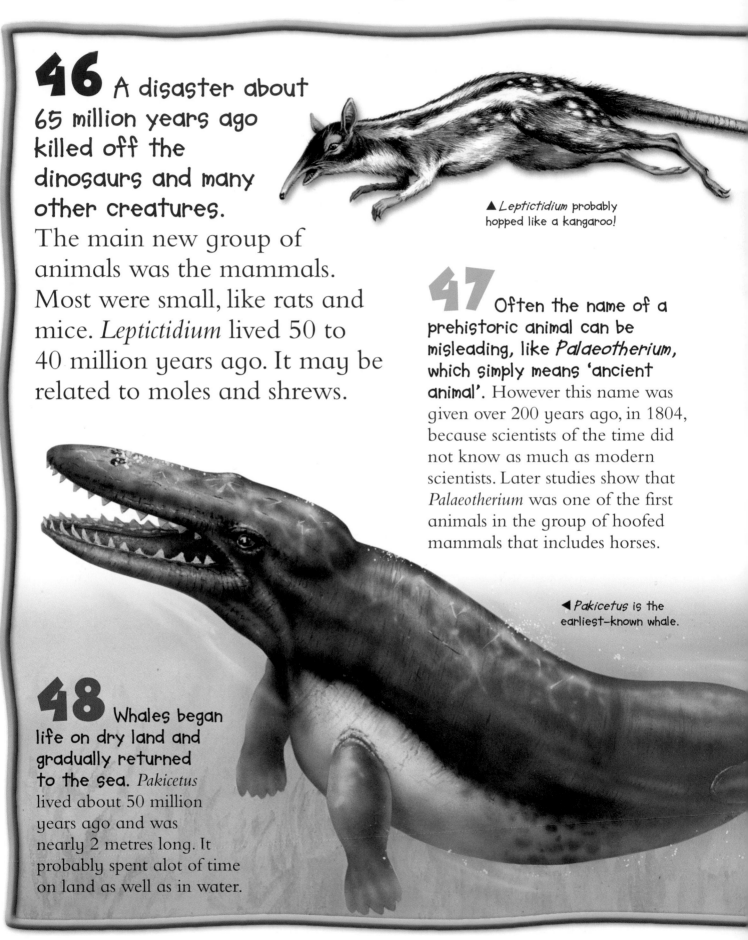

46 A disaster about 65 million years ago killed off the dinosaurs and many other creatures. The main new group of animals was the mammals. Most were small, like rats and mice. *Leptictidium* lived 50 to 40 million years ago. It may be related to moles and shrews.

▲ *Leptictidium* probably hopped like a kangaroo!

47 Often the name of a prehistoric animal can be misleading, like *Palaeotherium*, which simply means 'ancient animal'. However this name was given over 200 years ago, in 1804, because scientists of the time did not know as much as modern scientists. Later studies show that *Palaeotherium* was one of the first animals in the group of hoofed mammals that includes horses.

◄ *Pakicetus* is the earliest-known whale.

48 Whales began life on dry land and gradually returned to the sea. *Pakicetus* lived about 50 million years ago and was nearly 2 metres long. It probably spent alot of time on land as well as in water.

▼ A mother *Uintatherium* and her baby. This strange-looking creature was the largest land animal of its time. Its head was covered in horns and it had small tusks.

49 Around 40 million years ago, the largest animal walking the Earth was *Uintatherium*. This plant eater was over 3 metres long and nearly 2 metres tall at the shoulder – about the same size as a cow. Its fossils were found near the Uinta River in Colorado, USA. *Uintatherium* is thought to be a cousin of horses and elephants.

50 An animal's looks can be misleading. *Patriofelis* means 'father of the cats'. It lived 45 million years ago and was named because scientists thought it was an early cat. Later they realized that it merely looked like a cat. It was really a member of an extinct group of hunting animals called creodonts.

QUIZ
1. What does the name *Patriofelis* mean?
2. How long was *Pakicetus*?
3. In what year were *Palaeotherium* fossils found?
4. How tall was *Uintatherium*?
5. When did dinosaurs die out and mammals start to take over?

Answers:
1. 'Father of the cats' 2. About 2 metres 3. 1804 4. Almost 2 metres tall at the shoulder 5. 65 million years ago

As the world cooled down

51 Before the world started to cool 30 million years ago, palm trees grew almost everywhere – but they became rare. These trees had thrived in warm, wet conditions. But as Earth cooled, other plants took over, such as magnolias, pines, oaks and birch. These changes meant that animals changed too.

▼ *Brontotherium* was somewhere in size between a rhino and an elephant. Males used the Y-shaped horn on their snouts in fighting competitions.

52 *Pyrotherium* means 'fire beast', but not because this plant eater could walk through fire. Its fossils were found in layers of ash from an ancient volcano in Argentina, South America. The volcano probably erupted, and its fumes and ash suffocated and burned all the animals nearby. *Pyrotherium* was about as big as a cow and looked like a combination of a pig and a short-tusked elephant.

53 Many prehistoric animals have exciting names – *Brontotherium* means 'thunder beast'. Where the fossils of *Brontotherium* were found in North America, local people thought they were bones of the gods. They thought that these gods rode chariots across the sky and started thunderstorms, which led to the animal's name.

54 *Andrewsarchus* was a real big-head! At one metre long, it had the biggest head of any hunting mammal on land, and its strong jaws were filled with sharp, pointed teeth. Its whole body was bigger than a tiger of today. *Andrewsarchus* probably lived like a hyena, crunching up bones and gristle from dead animals. Yet it belonged to a mammal group that was mostly plant eaters. It lived 30 million years ago in what is now the deserts of Mongolia, Asia.

▲ *Andrewsarchus* was the biggest meat-eating land animal ever to have lived.

▼ The horns on *Arsinoitherium's* head were hollow and may have been used to make mating calls.

QUIZ
1. What does *Brontotherium* mean?
2. What does *Pyrotherium* mean?
3. How long was the head of *Andrewsarchus*?
4. Where did *Arsinoitherium* live?

Answers:
1. 'Thunder beast' 2. 'Fire beast' 3. One metre 4. Northern Africa

55 Some animals had horns as tall as people! *Arsinoitherium's* two massive horns looked like powerful weapons – but they were light, fragile and made of very thin bone. This plant eater lived in northern Africa about 35 million years ago. It was almost as big as an elephant and may have been an ancient cousin of the elephant group.

What fossils tell us

56 Fossils are the remains of animals or plants that have been preserved in rock. Usually only the hard parts of an animal, such as teeth or bones, are preserved in this way. Trilobites had a tough, outer skeleton so usually only this part of their body is found as a fossil. Scientists use the fossil to try to create a picture of how the soft parts, such as muscles and organs, may have looked.

▼ Some early humans are known only from their fossil footprints, not from fossils of their bones. These footprints were discovered in 1978 in Tanzania, Africa.

▲ By examining trilobite fossils, scientists were able to tell that this animal could see in all directions.

57 Some fossils are known as trace fossils. These are not fossilized parts of an animal's body, such as bones, but preserved marks left behind by the animal, such as footprints or droppings. By studying the fossilized footprints of an extinct animal, scientists can discover how it walked, how fast it could move and whether it lived alone or in groups.

58

On rare occasions the softer parts of an animal may be preserved as well as the hard parts. Insects may become trapped in sticky sap oozing from pine trees. This sap may then become fossilized as amber, with the insect caught inside. Scientists have found hundreds of insects, spiders and other small creatures perfectly preserved in this way.

▲ Amber spider fossils show that spiders have changed little over the last 30 million years.

QUIZ

1. What is a fossil?
2. What could scientists tell from trilobite fossils?
3. What is amber?
4. What animals did *Archaeopteryx* look like?

Answers:
1. Remains of animals or plants preserved in rock 2. That they could see in all directions 3. Fossil tree sap 4. A bird and a dinosaur

◄ Some fossils of *Archaeopteryx* are so well preserved that even the feathers can be seen.

59

One of the most important and valuable fossils ever found was of *Archaeopteryx*, in Germany in 1860. The fossil is about 150 million years old and shows a creature that looked part dinosaur and part bird. It had the feathers and wings of a bird, but the teeth and bony tail of a dinosaur. This shows that birds probably evolved from a type of dinosaur.

60

The importance of some fossils can be misunderstood. *Acanthostega* was one of the very earliest amphibian fossils ever found. However, the man who found the fossil was not an expert on amphibians. When his expedition returned from Greenland, the fossil was put in a drawer at a museum. It was not until over 30 years later that an expert on amphibians happened to see the fossil and realized how important it was.

Prehistoric prowlers

61 Some animals probably ate just about anything. Entelodonts were pig-like animals that lived 25 million years ago. *Dinohyus* was one of the largest entelodonts. Its teeth were sharp and strong, and it had powerful jaw muscles. It ate almost anything from plants and seeds, to small animals.

62 Some predators (hunting animals) walked on tiptoe but others were flat-footed. Most mammal predators, such as cats and dogs, walk on the ends of their toes. This helps them to run faster. *Daphoenodon* walked on flat feet, like a bear. It is often called a 'bear-dog' as it looked like a dog but walked like a bear.

▶ *Dinohyus* lived in North America and grew to be about 3 metres long. Its powerful neck muscles and large canine teeth suggest it could have broken bones and eaten flesh.

63 Fossils can show if predators hunted by day or at night. *Plesictis* was 75 centimetres long and its fossils show it had large sockets (spaces) for its eyes. This means that it probably hunted at night. It also had sharp claws and a long tail, so it probably scampered through trees hunting birds and insects, gripping with its claws and balancing with its tail.

64 Some predators have changed very little over millions of years. *Potamotherium* was an early otter and lived in Europe 23 million years ago. It looked almost like the otters of today. Its shape was so well-suited to hunting fish in streams that it has hardly changed.

▲ *Potamotherium* had a bendy backbone to allow it to twist about in the water.

QUIZ

1. Why is *Daphoenodon* sometimes called a 'bear-dog'?

2. Which hunter was active at night?

3. What prey did *Potamotherium* eat?

4. What do scientists think *Entelodon* ate?

Answers:
1. Because it looked like a dog, but walked like a bear 2. *Plesictis* 3. Fish 4. Almost anything

Amazing ancient elephants

65 The first elephant had tiny tusks and almost no trunk. *Moeritherium* lived in northern Africa about 36 million years ago. It stood just 60 centimetres tall and may have weighed around 20 kilograms – about the size of a large pet dog.

I DON'T BELIEVE IT!

The tusks of *Anancus* were over 4 metres long – almost as long as the animal itself.

▶ Woolly mammoths had coats of shaggy hair. This hair kept their warm inner fur dry and waterproof in the freezing conditions of the ice age.

66 Some elephants were very hairy. The woolly mammoth was covered in thick, long dense hair to keep out the cold of the ice age. It was larger than a modern elephant and was probably hunted by early people. The last woolly mammoths may have died out less than 10,000 years ago.

67 One elephant had tusks like shovels. *Platybelodon* lived about nine million years ago in Europe, Asia and Africa. Its lower tusks were shaped like broad, flat shovels. Perhaps it used them to scoop up water plants to eat.

68 **Some elephants had four tusks.** *Tetralophodon* lived about eight million years ago and stood 3 metres tall. Its fossils have been found in Europe, Asia, Africa and America, so it was a very widespread and successful animal.

69 **The biggest elephant was the Columbian mammoth.** It stood 4 metres tall and may have weighed over 10 tonnes – twice as much as most elephants today. It lived on the grasslands of southern North America.

▼ The Columbian mammoth had tusks that twisted into curved, spiral shapes.

70 **Elephants were more varied and common long ago, than they are today.** *Anancus* roamed Europe and Asia two million years ago. Like modern elephants, it used its trunk to pull leaves from branches and its tusks to dig up roots. However most kinds of prehistoric elephants died out. Only two kinds survive today, in Africa and Asia.

Animals with hooves

71 The first horse was hardly larger than a pet cat. *Hyracotherium* lived in Europe, Asia and North America about 50 million years ago. It was 20 centimetres tall and lived in woods and forests.

▲ *Hyracotherium* is sometimes called *Eohippus*, which means 'dawn horse'. It had a short neck, slender legs and a long tail.

72 Early horses did not eat grass – because there wasn't any. Grasses and open plains did not appear on Earth until 25 million years ago. Then early horses moved onto them, started to eat grass, and gradually became bigger.

73 Over millions of years, horses gradually lost their toes! The very first horses had five toes per foot, each ending in a small nail-like hoof. *Hyracotherium* had four toes on each front foot and three on each back foot. Later, *Mesohippus*, which was as big as a labrador dog, had three toes on each foot. Today's horses have just one toe on each foot, which ends in a large hoof.

74 Some prehistoric camels had horns. *Synthetoceras* had a pair of horns at the top of its head, and also an extraordinary Y-shaped horn growing from its nose. It probably used these horns to fight enemies and also to show off to others of its kind at breeding time.

▶ The amazing nose horn of *Synthetoceras* was present only on male animals.

HORSE RACE

You will need:
stiff card   crayons
scissors   string
about 4 metres long

On the card, draw a picture of *Hyracotherium*. Colour it in and cut it out. Make a hole in the middle, about 2 centimetres from the top. Thread the string through the hole and tie one end to a piece of furniture. Pull the string tight, then flick it with a finger to make *Hyracotherium* move along!

◀ *Megaloceros* may have stored food for the winter in the form of fat in a hump on its shoulder.

75 Some prehistoric deer had antlers as big as a person! *Megaloceros* means 'big deer' and it was as big as today's biggest deer, the moose. But its antlers were even bigger, measuring almost 4 metres from tip to tip. *Megaloceros* may have survived in some parts of Europe until as little as 3000 years ago.

Cats, dogs and bears

76 The sabre-tooth 'tiger' *Smilodon* had two huge sharp teeth like sabres (swords) – but it was not really a tiger. It belonged to a different group of cats to real tigers. *Smilodon*'s teeth were long and sharp but not very strong. It probably used them like knives to stab and slash at its prey, which then bled to death. *Smilodon* then ate it without a struggle.

▶ *Smilodon* had enormously powerful shoulders, so it may have sprung on its prey and held it down.

77 The earliest cats were similar to those of today. *Dinictis* lived about 30 million years ago and was strong and stealthy, like the modern-day cougar (mountain lion). It probably hunted like modern cats too, by creeping up close to a victim, then leaping on it to bite its throat or neck.

78 The first dog, *Hesperocyon*, had a long body and short legs, more like a stoat or mongoose. It was about 90 centimetres long and lived about 30 million years ago. Only later dogs had long legs and were able to run fast after their prey.

◀ *Hesperocyon* may have hunted in packs. This would have allowed it to hunt animals much larger than itself.

79 The sabre-tooth 'cat' *Thylacosmilus* was not even a real cat! It had a cat-shaped head, body, legs and tail. Yet it was a marsupial – a cousin of kangaroos and koalas. It lived in South America four million years ago.

80 Sea lions did not develop from lions – but from dogs. *Allodesmus* was an early type of sea lion and lived about 13 million years ago. It had strong flippers for fast swimming. Its fossil bones show that it came originally from the dog group.

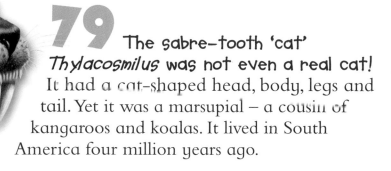

I DON'T BELIEVE IT!

Even if global warming continues, the world will not be as hot us it was 35 million years ago.

◀ Early humans had to face many natural dangers, such as cave bears.

81 Early people hunted cave bears, and cave bears hunted early people! The huge cave bear of the Ice Age was as big as today's grizzly bear. Humans called Neanderthals hunted them and used their bones and teeth as ornaments. The bears hunted people too, and left their bones in caves.

Prehistoric giants

82 **The largest flying bird ever was as big as a small plane!** *Argentavis* was twice the size of any flying bird today. Its wings measured 7 metres from tip to tip. It was a huge vulture that fed on the dead bodies of other creatures, tearing off their flesh with its powerful hooked beak.

▼ *Argentavis* lived about seven million years ago in South America.

83 **Some birds were even bigger than *Argentavis*, but they could not fly — and they were deadly hunters.** In South America about one million years ago, *Titanis* grew to 3 metres tall. It raced after its prey, which it tore apart with its huge, hooked beak.

▶ in South America, *Titanis* was a monstrous hunting bird that chased after mammals such as this early horse.

84 **A type of prehistoric kangaroo, *Procoptodon*, was twice as big as those of today.** Yet it could bound along as fast as a racehorse. Like kangaroos of today, it was a marsupial, carrying its baby in a pouch. It lived in Australia.

85 The largest land mammal ever to have lived was a type of rhino – without a nose horn. *Paraceratherium* was far bigger than an elephant, at 8 metres long and 6 metres tall at the shoulder. It weighed over 15 tonnes – more than three elephants. This giant creature lived in Asia about 30 million years ago and was a peaceful plant eater.

I DON'T BELIEVE IT!
Giant marsupials may have started stories of the 'Bunyip', a mythical Australian animal.

▲ The huge *Paraceratherium* fed by browsing on trees, stripping off the leaves. Even though it was so big and heavy, *Paraceratherium* had long legs, which means it was probably capable of running.

A giant island

86 For almost 50 million years, South America was like a giant island – with many strange animals that were found nowhere else. Until three million years ago, South America was separated from North America by an ocean. On islands, animals can evolve into unusual kinds found nowhere else in the world.

▶ South America was once separated from North America. This meant that certain animals that survived there, such as *Macrauchenia* and *Glyptodon*, did not live anywhere else in the world.

87 Elephants were not the only animals with trunks! *Macrauchenia* lived in South America about 100,000 years ago. It was about the size of a camel and probably had a trunk to gather leaves to eat. It was not a type of elephant, but a distant cousin of horses and rhinos.

88 Armadillos were once nearly as big as tanks! *Glyptodon* was almost 4 metres long and covered in a thick dome of bony armour. It lived in South America until about 10,000 years ago. Today, armadillos are quite small, but they are still covered in bony plates for protection.

Macrauchenia

Glyptodon

89 One South American creature that died out was the giant sloth, *Megatherium*. It was a cousin of the smaller sloths that live in trees today – but it was far too big to climb trees. At 6 metres long and 3 tonnes in weight, it was the size of an elephant!

90 When South America joined North America, many kinds of prehistoric animals died out. In particular, animals from North America spread south. They were better at surviving than the South American creatures, and they gradually took over.

▶ *Megatherium* may only have died out in the last few thousand years.

I DON'T BELIEVE IT!
The armadillo is a South American animal that lives in North America, too. Over the past 100 years, it has spread north at a rate of one kilometre every ten years.

Our prehistoric relations

91 Monkeys, apes and humans first appeared over 50 million years ago – and the first kinds looked like squirrels. This group is called the primates. *Plesiadapis* was one of the first primates. It lived 55 million years ago in Europe and North America.

◀ *Plesiadapis* had claws on its fingers and toes, unlike monkeys and apes, which had nails.

92 Early apes walked on all fours. About 20 million years ago, *Dryopithecus* lived in Europe and Asia. It used its arms and legs to climb trees. When it came down to the ground, it walked on all fours. It was 60 centimetres long and ate fruit and leaves.

▶ The early ape *Dryopithecus* walked flat on its feet, unlike other apes, which walked on their knuckles.

I DON'T BELIEVE IT

The first fossils of the giant ape *Gigantopithecus* to be studied by scientists came from a second-hand shop in Hong Kong, over 70 years ago.

▼ The need to see longer distances on grasslands may have caused the first apes to walk on two legs.

93 **Some kinds of apes may have walked on their two back legs, like us.** About 4.5 million years ago *Ardipithecus* lived in Africa. Only a few of its fossils have been found. However, experts think it may have walked upright on its back legs. It could have made the first steps in the change, or evolution, from apes to humans.

94 **One prehistoric ape was a real giant – it was more than 3 metres tall!** Its name, *Gigantopithecus*, means 'giant ape'. It was much larger than today's biggest ape, the gorilla, which grows up to 2 metres tall. *Gigantopithecus* probably ate roots and seeds, and may have hunted small animals such as birds, rats and lizards.

► The enormous *Gigantopithecus* could probably stand on its hind legs to reach food.

95 **Scientists work out which animals are our closest cousins partly from fossils – and also from chemicals.** The chemical called DNA contains genes, which are instructions for how living things grow and work. The living animals with DNA most similar to ours are the great apes, chimpanzees and gorillas, both from Africa. So our ancient cousins were probably apes like them. The orang-utan, from Southeast Asia, is less similar.

The first humans

▼ *Australopithecus* walked upright. It spent most of its days searching for food.

96 Our early prehistoric cousins were much smaller than us. One kind was called *Australopithecus afarensis*, meaning 'southern ape from Afar', because its fossils come from the Afar region of East Africa. It was just over one metre tall, lived over three million years ago, and looked part human and part ape.

▶ *Homo erectus* was the first living creature to use fire for cooking and warmth.

97 Very early kinds of humans lived almost two million years ago. They were called *Homo erectus*, which means 'upright human', and they were as tall as us. These first humans spread from Africa, across Asia, and into Europe. However, they all died out about 200,000 years ago.

98 From one million years ago early people made tools out of stone — they had not invented metal. They chipped rocks like flint to form a sharp, cutting edge, and shaped stones into knives, scrapers, or axes. Stone tools have been found with the bones of animals that were cut up for food, along with the ashes of fires used for cooking — and the bones of the people themselves.

▶ The Flores humans probably used stone tools to hunt animals such as the pygmy elephant.

99 **Some prehistoric animals were domesticated (tamed) to become the first farm animals.** This began around 15,000 years ago. For example, fierce aurochs, a type of wild cow, were gradually bred over time to become quiet, calm animals. They provided people with food and clothing.

100 **We are still discovering surprises about prehistoric life.** In 2004, scientists found the bones and tools of tiny humans, less than one metre tall, on the island of Flores in Southeast Asia. Their remains are from over 90,000 to less than 15,000 years old. No one knew they existed. In the future we may discover more amazing finds from the past.

QUIZ

1. Were prehistoric humans big or small?

2. What were the first tools made from?

3. When were animals first domesticated?

4. What was discovered on the island of Flores?

Answers:
1. Small 2. Stone 3. 15,000 years ago 4. Flores man

DINOSAURS

101 **For more than 160 million years, dinosaurs ruled the land.** There were many different kinds – huge and tiny, tall and short, slim and bulky, fast and slow, with fierce sharp-toothed meat-eaters and peacefully munching plant-eaters. Then a great disaster ended their rule.

▼ In South America 70 million years ago, a group of *Austroraptor* dinosaurs attack a huge plant-eater. Many fast, fierce 'raptor' dinosaurs had feathers. *Austroraptor* was one of the largest raptors at 300-plus kilograms and 5 metres long.

When were dinosaurs alive?

102 The Age of Dinosaurs lasted from about 230 million to 65 million years ago, during a time called the Mesozoic Era. Dinosaurs were the main creatures on land for 80 times longer than people have been on Earth!

▼ Towards the end of the Palaeozoic Era, reptiles replaced amphibians as the main large land animals. Dinosaurs were in turn replaced in the Cenozoic Era by mammals. MYA means million years ago.

103 Dinosaurs were not the only animals living in the Mesozoic Era. There were many other kinds such as insects, spiders, shellfish, fish, scurrying lizards, crocodiles and furry mammals.

104 There were different shapes and sizes of dinosaurs. Some were small enough to hold in your hand. Others were bigger than a house!

◄ Tiny *Saltopus*, less than one metre long, was a Triassic close cousin of dinosaurs.

PALAEOZOIC ERA

The reptiles, including the ancestors of the dinosaurs, start to become more dominant than the amphibians.

Lystrosaurus (amphibian)

Diplocaulus (mammal-like reptile)

299–251 MYA
PERMIAN PERIOD

MESOZOIC ERA

The first true dinosaurs appear. These are small two-legged carnivores (meat-eaters), and larger herbivores, or plant-eaters.

Procompsognathus

Riojasaurus

251–200 MYA
TRIASSIC PERIOD

Many different dinosaurs lived at this time, including the giant plant-eaters such as *Barosaurus*.

Barosaurus

Allosaurus

200–145.5 MYA
JURASSIC PERIOD

◀ *Stegosaurus* thrived during the late Jurassic Period, in North America and Europe.

106

There were no people during the Age of Dinosaurs. There was a gap of more than 60 million years between the last dinosaurs and the first humans.

105

No single kind of dinosaur survived for all of the Mesozoic Era. Many different types came and went. Some lasted for less than a million years. Other kinds, like *Stegosaurus*, kept going for many millions of years.

I DON'T BELIEVE IT!

The name 'dinosaur' means 'terrible lizard'. But dinosaurs weren't lizards, and not all dinosaurs were terrible. Small plant-eating dinosaurs were about as 'terrible' as today's sheep!

MESOZOIC ERA

During the last part of the Age of Dinosaurs, both giant carnivores and armoured herbivores were alive.

Tyrannosaurus rex

Deinonychus

Saltasaurus

Spinosaurus

145.5–65.5 MYA CRETACEOUS PERIOD

CENOZOIC ERA

The dinosaurs have died out, and large mammals soon take over the land.

Megacerops **herbivorous mammal**

Nesodon **herbivorous mammal**

Newer kinds of mammals become more common, such as cats, horses, whales and bats.

Thylacosmilus **carnivorous mammal**

65.5–23 MYA PALEOGENE PERIOD

23–2.6 MYA NEOGENE PERIOD

Before the dinosaurs

107 Dinosaurs were not the first animals on Earth. Many other kinds of creatures lived before them, including different types of reptiles – the group that includes dinosaurs.

▶ *Erythrosuchus* was a crocodile-like reptile that lived before dinosaurs were common.

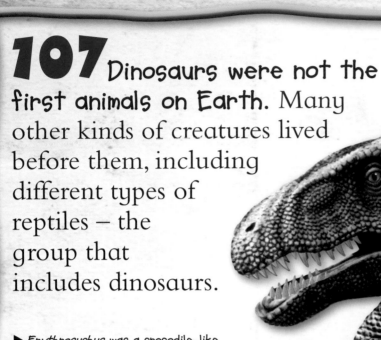

108 *Dimetrodon* was a fierce, meat-eating reptile. Although it looked like a dinosaur it wasn't one. It lived 270 million years ago, well before the dinosaurs arrived. *Dimetrodon* was about 3 metres long and had a tall flap of skin like a sail on its back.

▶ *Dimetrodon*'s legs sprawled sideways from its body, like a lizard, rather than being underneath, as in dinosaurs.

109 Early crocodiles also looked like dinosaurs. Crocodiles were around even before the first dinosaurs. One was *Erythrosuchus*, which was 4.5 metres long, lived 240 million years ago, lurked in swamps and ate fish.

110 **Therapsids were around before the dinosaurs, and they also lived alongside the early dinosaurs.** They were mammal-like reptiles because they didn't have scaly skin like most reptiles. Instead they had furry or hairy skin like mammals.

111 **The dinosaur group probably appeared 238–232 million years ago.** Lack of fossils means no one is sure when, where, or what were the ancestors. However it is known that the dinosaurs' closest relations include crocodiles and the flying reptiles called pterosaurs, all making up the bigger group termed archosaurs.

▶ *Euparkeria* could probably rear up to run on just its two rear legs — like many meat-eating dinosaurs later.

112 **Some small reptiles show what the dinosaurs' ancestors could have looked like.** They include *Euparkeria* in South Africa 245 million years ago, and *Lagosuchus* and *Marasuchus* in South America around 235 million years ago. They were small, light and fast, with long back legs, and sharp teeth for feeding on bugs and small creatures.

55

Dinosaurs arrive

113 The earliest dinosaurs stalked the Earth almost 230 million years ago. They lived in what is now Argentina, in South America. They included *Eoraptor* and *Herrerasaurus*. Both were slim and fast creatures. They could stand almost upright and run on their two rear legs. Few other animals of the time could run upright like this, on legs that were straight below their bodies. Most other animals had legs that stuck out sideways.

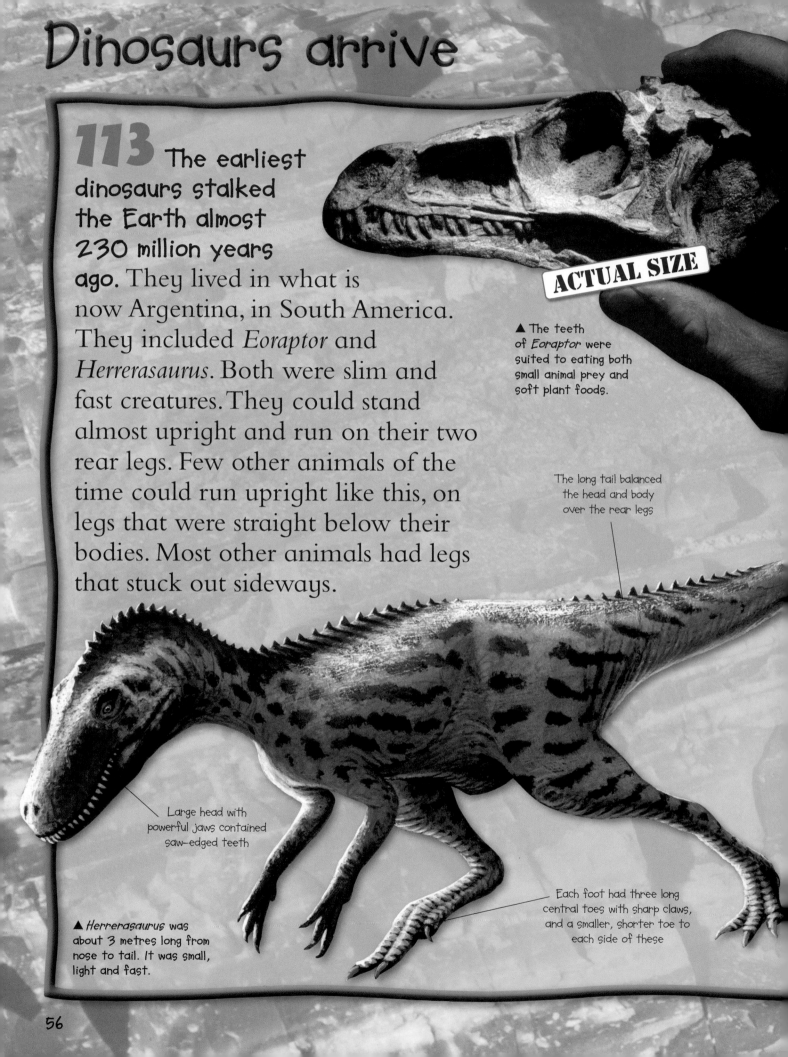

ACTUAL SIZE

▲ The teeth of *Eoraptor* were suited to eating both small animal prey and soft plant foods.

The long tail balanced the head and body over the rear legs

Large head with powerful jaws contained saw-edged teeth

▲ *Herrerasaurus* was about 3 metres long from nose to tail. It was small, light and fast.

Each foot had three long central toes with sharp claws, and a smaller, shorter toe to each side of these

56

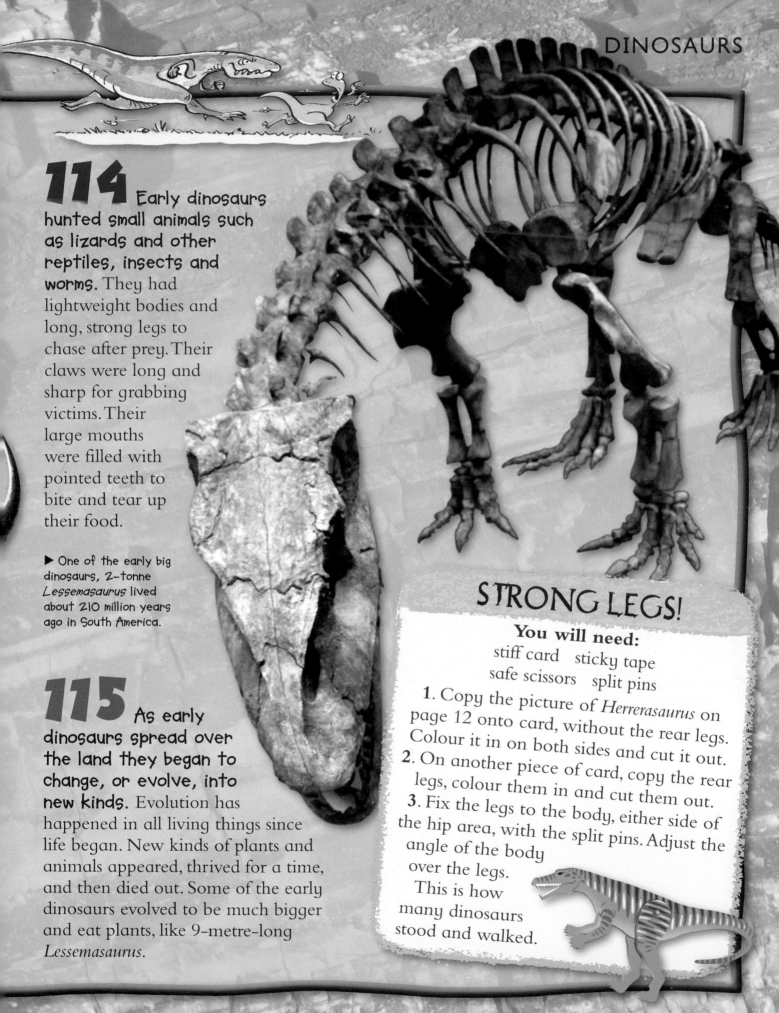

114 Early dinosaurs hunted small animals such as lizards and other reptiles, insects and worms. They had lightweight bodies and long, strong legs to chase after prey. Their claws were long and sharp for grabbing victims. Their large mouths were filled with pointed teeth to bite and tear up their food.

▶ One of the early big dinosaurs, 2-tonne *Lessemasaurus* lived about 210 million years ago in South America.

115 As early dinosaurs spread over the land they began to change, or evolve, into new kinds. Evolution has happened in all living things since life began. New kinds of plants and animals appeared, thrived for a time, and then died out. Some of the early dinosaurs evolved to be much bigger and eat plants, like 9-metre-long *Lessemasaurus*.

STRONG LEGS!

You will need:
stiff card   sticky tape
safe scissors   split pins

1. Copy the picture of *Herrerasaurus* on page 12 onto card, without the rear legs. Colour it in on both sides and cut it out.
2. On another piece of card, copy the rear legs, colour them in and cut them out.
3. Fix the legs to the body, either side of the hip area, with the split pins. Adjust the angle of the body over the legs.

This is how many dinosaurs stood and walked.

First of the giants

116 One of the first big dinosaurs well-known from fossils was *Plateosaurus*. This plant-eater grew up to 8 metres long and lived almost 220 million years ago in what is now Europe. It could rear up on its back legs and use its long neck to reach food high in trees.

Long, flexible neck for reaching food high off the ground

Sharp, jabbing claws for defence

Long, strong tail for balance

Powerful back legs for rearing up

▲ Fossils of more than 100 *Plateosaurus* have been found, so its size, shape, teeth and body details are well known compared to many other dinosaurs.

Small head and long, flexible neck

117 *Riojasaurus* was an even larger plant-eater. It lived 218 million years ago in what is now Argentina. *Riojasaurus* was 10 metres long and weighed over one tonne – as much as a large family car of today.

118 The first big plant-eating dinosaurs may have become larger, with longer necks, so that they could reach up into trees for food. Their great size would also have helped them fight enemies, since many other big meat-eating reptiles, some as long as 5 metres, were ready to make a meal of them.

◄ Like *Plateosaurus*, *Riojasaurus* was in the dinosaur group called prosauropods, with a small head, long neck and long tail.

119 These early dinosaurs lived during the first part of the Age of Dinosaurs – the Triassic Period. By its end, 200 million years ago, dozens of kinds of dinosaurs roamed across much of the world.

I DON'T BELIEVE IT!

Early plant-eating dinosaurs did not eat fruits or grasses – there weren't any! They hadn't appeared yet. Instead they ate plants called horsetails, ferns, cycads and conifer trees.

What teeth tell us

120 We know about dinosaurs and other living things from long ago because of fossils. These are usually hard body parts, such as bones, claws, horns and scales, that are preserved in rocks for millions of years. Dinosaur teeth were very hard and formed many fossils.

122 The shape of a dinosaur's teeth help to show what it ate. *Edmontosaurus* was a 12-metre-long duck-billed dinosaur, and had rows of broad, wide, sharp-ridged teeth in the sides of its mouth. These were ideal for chewing tough plant foods like twigs and old leaves.

◄ The head of *Edmontosaurus* was long, broad and muscular, suited to spending hours chewing — similar to today's horse.

Toothless beak-like front of mouth

More than 500 chewing back teeth

121 *Tyrannosaurus* had 50–60 long, pointed teeth more than 20 centimetres long. These were excellent for tearing up victims, and for ripping off lumps of flesh for swallowing. As in other dinosaurs, all through life as old teeth broke or fell out, new ones grew in their place.

► *Tyrannosaurus* teeth were strong and stout, but not especially sharp-edged, more suited to tearing than slicing.

123 Some dinosaurs, such as *Gallimimus*, had no teeth at all! The mouth was shaped like a bird's beak and made of a tough, strong, horny substance like our fingernails. The beak was suited to pecking up all kinds of foods like seeds, worms and bugs, as many birds do today.

▲ *Gallimimus* was a type of 'ostrich dinosaur' with large eyes, a long, lightweight beak and long neck.

124 *Baryonyx* had narrow, pointed, cone-shaped teeth. These resemble the teeth of a crocodile or dolphin today. They were ideal for grabbing slippery prey such as fish.

▲ The head of *Baryonyx* was more than one metre long, with an expanded, spoon-shaped front snout.

125 The teeth of the giant, long-necked dinosaur *Apatosaurus* were shaped like pencils. They worked like a rake to pull leaves off branches into the mouth, for the dinosaur to swallow.

DINOSAUR TEETH!

With the help of an adult, look in a utensils drawer or tool box for dinosaur teeth! Some tools resemble the teeth of some dinosaurs, and do similar jobs.
File or rasp – broad surface with hard ridges, like the plant-chewing teeth of *Edmontosaurus*.
Knife – long and pointed, like the meat-tearing teeth of *Tyrannosaurus rex*.
Pliers – Gripping and squeezing, like the beak-shaped mouth of *Gallimimus*.

▲ Although *Apatosaurus* was about 25 metres long, its skull measured just 60 centimetres. It spent most of its time feeding.

Super-size dinosaurs

126 **The true giants of the Age of Dinosaurs were the sauropods.** These vast dinosaurs all had a small head, long neck, barrel-shaped body, long tapering tail and four pillar-like legs. The biggest sauropods included *Brachiosaurus*, *Mamenchisaurus*, *Barosaurus*, *Diplodocus*, *Futalognkosaurus* and *Argentinosaurus*.

◀ Fossil footprints from a sauropod herd near Purgatoire River, Colorado, USA.

127 **Sauropod dinosaurs probably lived in groups or herds.** We know this from their footprints, which have been preserved as fossils. Each foot left a print as large as a chair seat. Hundreds of footprints together showed many sauropods walked along with each other.

▲ *Futalognkosaurus*, a type of sauropod known as a titanosaur, was more than 30 metres long. Its name, given in 2007, means 'giant chief lizard' in the local Argentinian language.

Diplodocus is also known as 'Old Whip-tail'! It may have swished its long tail so hard and fast that it made an enormous CRACK like a whip. This living, leathery, scaly whip would scare away enemies or even rip off their skin.

128 **Sauropod dinosaurs swallowed pebbles – on purpose!** Their peg-like teeth could only rake in plant food, not chew it. Pebbles and stones gulped into the stomach helped to grind and crush the food. These pebbles, smooth and polished by the grinding, have been found with the fossil bones of sauropods.

▶ *Brachiosaurus* was about 25 metres long and probably weighed in the region of 30 tonnes. Its amazingly long neck allowed it to browse from the tallest trees.

129 **The biggest sauropods like *Brachiosaurus* and *Futalognkosaurus* were enormous beasts.** They weighed up to ten times more than elephants of today. Yet their fossil footprints showed they could run quite fast – nearly as quickly as you!

130 **Sauropods probably had to eat most of the time, 20 hours out of every 24.** They had enormous bodies that would need great amounts of food, but only small mouths to gather the food.

Killer claws

131 Nearly all dinosaurs had claws on their fingers and toes. These claws were shaped for different jobs in different dinosaurs. They were made from a tough substance called keratin – the same as your fingernails and toenails.

132 *Hypsilophodon* had strong, sturdy claws. This small 2-metre-long plant-eater probably used them to scrabble and dig in soil for seeds and roots.

133 *Deinonychus* had long, hooked claws on its hands. These helped it to grab victims and tear at their skin and flesh. It also had a huge hooked claw, as big as your hand, on the second toe of each foot. This could flick down like a pointed knife to slash pieces out of prey.

◀ *Deinonychus*, meaning 'terrible claw', probably had feathers like other raptors. It lived in North America 110 million years ago.

Long claw on each of the three fingers

Second toe had slashing 'terrible claw'

134 *Baryonyx* also had a large claw, but this was on the thumb of each hand. It may have worked as a fish hook to snatch fish from water.

135 *Iguanodon* had claws on its feet. But these were rounded and blunt and looked more like hooves. There were also stubby claws on the fingers, while the thumb claw was longer and shaped like a spike, perhaps for stabbing enemies.

▶ Therizinosaurs, from the Cretaceous Period in Eastern Asia and Western North America, had enormous finger claws — why is a mystery.

136 Giant sauropod dinosaurs had almost flat claws. Dinosaurs such as *Apatosaurus* looked like they had toenails on their huge feet!

▶ The long claw on *Apatosaurus*' front foot was possibly for self defence.

137 The biggest claws of any dinosaurs, and any animals, belonged to the scythe dinosaurs or therizinosaurs. Their hand claws, up to one metre long, were perhaps used to pull down and cut off leafy branches as food.

138 Therizinosaurs were big, strange-looking dinosaurs, reaching 10 metres long and 5 tonnes in weight. They lived late in the Age of Dinosaurs, and the group included *Alxasaurus*, *Nothronychus*, *Beipiaosaurus* and *Therizinosaurus*.

Deadly meat-eaters

Spinosaurus lived about 100 million years ago. It grew to 15 metres in length, and weighed as much as 10 tonnes.

About 13–14 metres in length, Carcharodontosaurus hunted across North Africa 95 million years ago. Its saw-edged teeth were 20 centimetres long.

Giganotosaurus was up to 13.5 metres long and had the largest skull of any meat-eating dinosaur. It lived about 97 million years ago.

139 The biggest meat-eating dinosaurs were the largest predators ever to walk on Earth. *Allosaurus*, which lived 150 million years ago in North America, reached almost 10 metres in length, while *Tyrannosaurus rex* from 66 million years ago was 12 metres. In South America, *Giganotosaurus* was slightly larger, while in North Africa, *Carcharodontosaurus* and *Spinosaurus* were even bigger – the largest meat-eating dinosaurs known so far.

140 These great predators were well equipped for hunting large prey — including other dinosaurs. They had massive mouths with long sharp teeth in powerful jaws. They also had long, strong back legs to run fast, and enormous toe claws for kicking and holding down victims.

141 Meat-eaters probably got food in various ways. They hid behind rocks or trees and rushed out to surprise a victim. Some chased their prey, and others would plod steadily over time to tire out their meal. They might even scavenge — feast on the bodies of creatures that were dead or dying from old age, illness or injury.

T rex was among the last of the great predatory dinosaurs. It probably weighed 6–7 tonnes when fully grown.

Allosaurus was the largest meat-eating dinosaur of the Jurassic Period. It was a relative lightweight at only 2–3 tonnes!

Look! Listen! Sniff!

142 Like the reptiles of today, dinosaurs could see, hear and smell the world around them. We know this from fossils. The preserved fossil skulls had spaces for eyes, ears and nostrils.

143 Some dinosaurs, such as *Leaellynasaura* and *Troodon*, had big eyes. There are large, bowl-shaped hollows in their fossil skulls to allow for them. Today, animals such as mice, owls and night-time lizards can see well in the dark. Perhaps *Troodon* prowled through the forest at night, peering in the gloom for small creatures to eat.

▶ *Leaellynasaura*, was a 3-metre-long plant-eater from 115 million years ago in what is now Australia.

▶ *Troodon* was about 2 metres long and lived in North America 70 million years ago.

144 There are also spaces on the sides of the head where *Troodon* had its ears. Dinosaur ears were round and flat, like the ears of other reptiles. *Troodon* could hear the tiny noises of little animals moving about in the dark.

145 The nostrils of *Troodon*, where it breathed in air and smelled scents, were two holes at the front of its snout. With its delicate sense of smell, *Troodon* could sniff out its prey of insects, worms, little reptiles such as lizards, and small shrew-like mammals.

146 Dinosaurs used their eyes, ears and noses not only to find food, but also to detect enemies – and each other. *Parasaurolophus* had a long, hollow, tube-like crest on its head. Perhaps it blew air along this to make a noise like a trumpet, as an elephant does today with its trunk.

147 Dinosaurs such as *Parasaurolophus* may have made noises to send messages to other members of their group or herd. Different messages could tell the others about finding food or warn them about enemies.

BIG EYES

You will need:
stiff card   safe scissors   elastic   colour pencils

1. Make a *Troodon* mask from card. Carefully cut out the shape as shown. Then cut out two small eye holes, each just 1 centimetre across. Colour in your mask
2. Attach elastic so you can wear the mask and find out how little you can see.
3. Make the eye holes as large as the eyes of the real *Troodon*. Now you can have a much bigger, clearer view of the world!

▼ *Parasaurolophus* was a 'duck-billed' dinosaur or hadrosaur. It was about 10 metres long and lived 80 million years ago in North America.

Living with dinosaurs

148 All dinosaurs walked and ran on land, as far as we know. No dinosaurs could fly in the air or spend their lives swimming in the water. But many other creatures, which lived at the same time as the dinosaurs, could fly or swim. Some were reptiles, like the dinosaurs.

149 Ichthyosaurs were reptiles that lived in the sea. They were shaped like dolphins, long and slim with fins and a tail. They chased after fish to eat.

150 Plesiosaurs were sea-dwelling reptiles. They had long necks, rounded bodies, four large flippers and a short tail.

151 Turtles were another kind of reptile that swam in the oceans long ago. Each had a strong, domed shell and four flippers. Turtles still survive today. However ichthyosaurs and then plesiosaurs died out by the end of the Age of Dinosaurs.

▶ In this marine and shoreline Cretaceous scene, the dinosaurs *Ouranosaurus* (4) are shown living alongside lots of other types of animals.

152
Pterosaurs were reptiles that could fly. They had thin, skin-like wings held out by long finger bones. Some soared over the sea and grabbed small fish in their sharp-toothed, beak-shaped mouths. Others swooped on small land animals.

153
Birds first appeared about 150 million years ago. Some evolved to dive for fish in the sea, like gulls and terns today. *Ichthyornis* was about 25 centimetres long and lived along North American coasts.

▲ Unlike modern birds, *Ichthyornis* had tiny teeth in its jaws to grip slippery prey.

Key
1 *Hesperornis* (flightless bird)
2 *Elasmosaurus* (marine reptile)
3 *Pteranodon* (flying reptile)
4 *Ouranosaurus* (dinosaur)
5 *Archelon* (turtle, laying eggs)
6 *Archelon* (turtle, swimming)
7 *Kronosaurus* (marine reptile)
8 *Ichthyosaurus* (marine reptile)
9 Belemnoid (mollusc, similar to modern squid
10 *Mosasaurus* (marine reptile)
11 *Elasmosaurus* (marine reptile)
12 Ammonoid (mollusc)
13 *Cretoxyrhina* (shark)

154
Mosasaurs were huge, fearsome reptiles that appeared later in the Age of Dinosaurs. Related to lizards, they had a massive mouth full of sharp teeth. Some grew to 13 metres long and weighed over 5 tonnes.

How fast?

155 Dinosaurs walked and ran at different speeds, according to their size and shape. In the world today, cheetahs and ostriches are slim with long legs and run very fast. Elephants and hippos are huge heavyweights and plod along more slowly. Dinosaurs were similar. Some were big, heavy and slow. Others were slim, light and speedy.

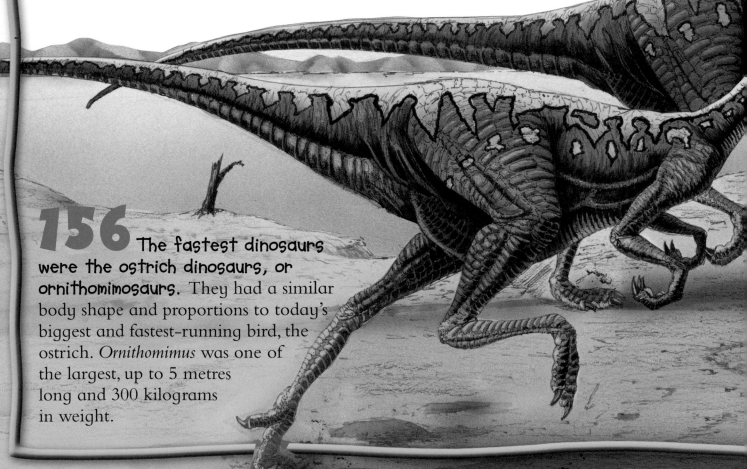

▼ *Ornithomimus*, from North America 70–65 million years ago, had long, powerful back legs, and hollow bones (like a bird) to save weight.

156 The fastest dinosaurs were the ostrich dinosaurs, or ornithomimosaurs. They had a similar body shape and proportions to today's biggest and fastest-running bird, the ostrich. *Ornithomimus* was one of the largest, up to 5 metres long and 300 kilograms in weight.

157 *Muttaburrasaurus* was a huge ornithopod type of dinosaur, a cousin of *Iguanodon*. It probably walked about as fast as you, around 4 to 5 kilometres an hour. It might have been able to gallop along at a top speed of 15 kilometres an hour, making the ground shake with its 3-tonne weight!

Ankle bones

Foot bones

▶ Fossils of *Muttaburrasaurus* come from Queensland, Australia. This bulky plant-eater had three large toes on each back foot and also three on the smaller front foot.

Toe bones ended in rounded claws

158 *Coelophysis* was a slim, lightweight dinosaur. It could probably trot, jump and dart about with great agility. Sometimes it ran upright on its two back legs. Or it could bound along on all fours like a dog at more than 30 kilometres an hour.

▼ *Coelophysis* was 3 metres long. It was one of the earliest dinosaurs, living about 220 million years ago.

Built like tanks

159 Some dinosaurs had body defences against predators. These might be large horns and spikes, or thick, hard lumps of bone like armour-plating. Most armoured dinosaurs were plant-eaters. They had to defend themselves against big meat-eating dinosaurs such as *Tyrannosaurus*.

160 *Triceratops* had three horns, one on its nose and two much longer ones above its eyes. It also had a wide shield-like piece of bone over its neck and shoulders. The horns and neck frill made *Triceratops* look very fearsome. But most of the time it quietly ate plants. If attacked, *Triceratops* could charge and jab with its horns, like a rhino today.

▼ *Triceratops* was 9 metres long and weighed more than 5 tonnes. It lived 65 million years ago in North America.

Wide neck frill of bone and skin

Long, sharp brow horns

Smaller nose horn

Sharp beak-shaped front of mouth

Wide feet spread great body weight

161

Styracosaurus was a ceratopsian ('horn–face') dinosaur, like *Triceratops*, but with a more elaborate neck frill. Up to six horns as long as one metre extended from the frill's edge, giving this dinosaur an even fiercer appearance.

DESIGN A DINOSAUR!

Make an imaginary dinosaur. It might have the body armour and tail club of *Euoplocephalus*, or the head horns and neck frill of *Triceratops*. You can draw your dinosaur, or make it out of pieces of card or from modelling clay. Give it a made-up name, like *Euoploceratops* or *Tricephalus*. How well protected is your dinosaur? How does it compare to some armoured creatures of today, such as tortoises, armadillos or porcupines?

Tail club made from several fused (joined) bones

Long, straight, powerful tail to swing club

▲ *Styracosaurus* grew up to 6 metres long and was 1.8 metres tall at the shoulder.

Back covered with bony plates set within the skin

162

Euoplocephalus had a great lump of bone on its tail. This measured almost one metre across and looked like a massive hammer or club. *Euoplocephalus* could swing it at predators to protect itself from attack.

◄ *Euoplocephalus* belonged to the group called ankylosaurs. With big bony sheets and lumps in their skin, they were the most armoured of all dinosaurs.

Nests and eggs

163 Like most reptiles today, dinosaurs produced young by laying eggs. These hatched out into baby dinosaurs that gradually grew into adults.

164 Many kinds of dinosaur eggs and babies have been found. These include those of small, strong-beaked *Oviraptor* from Central Asia and the early sauropod *Massospondylus* from South Africa.

▼ This female *Oviraptor* is checking the newly laid eggs in her nest. Each egg is 14–18 centimetres long.

165 Different dinosaurs laid different sizes and shapes of eggs. Huge sauropod dinosaurs such as *Brachiosaurus* probably laid rounded eggs as big as basketballs. Eggs of big meat-eaters like *Tyrannosaurus* were more sausage-shaped, 40 centimetres long and 15 centimetres wide.

166 Some dinosaurs made nests for their eggs. *Oviraptor* lived more than 75 million years ago in what is now the Gobi Desert of Asia. It probably scraped a bowl-shaped nest in the soil about one metre across. Into this it laid about 15–20 eggs, in a neat spiral shape.

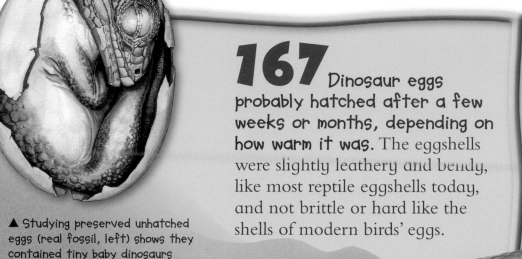

167 Dinosaur eggs probably hatched after a few weeks or months, depending on how warm it was. The eggshells were slightly leathery and bendy, like most reptile eggshells today, and not brittle or hard like the shells of modern birds' eggs.

▲ Studying preserved unhatched eggs (real fossil, left) shows they contained tiny baby dinosaurs (artist's drawing, right).

▶ Seventy-five million years ago in East Asia, pig-sized *Protoceratops* prepares to defend its nest and eggs from a hungry *Velociraptor*.

168 Fossils of baby dinosaurs show that they looked very much like their parents. However the neck frill of a baby *Protoceratops* was not as large when compared to the rest of its body, as in the adult. As the youngster's body grew, the frill grew faster, so its relative size changed. Other dinosaurs' body proportions also changed as they grew bigger.

169 Recent fossil finds show that some dinosaurs looked after their babies, like some reptiles today, such as crocodiles. In one discovery, an adult *Protoceratops* was preserved with some babies just 10–15 centimetres long, probably less than one year old.

Dinosaur babies

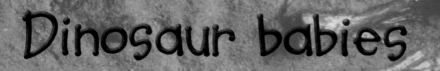

170 Some dinosaur parents may have fed their young. Fossils of duckbilled *Maiasaura* include nests, eggs and newly hatched young. The hatchlings could not move around because their leg bones were not strong enough. Yet their tiny teeth had slight scratches and other marks from eating food. So the parent *Maiasaura* probably brought food, such as leaves and berries, to the nest for them.

▼ In 1978 more than 200 fossils of *Maiasaura* nests, eggs, babies, youngsters and adults were found at a site now known as 'Egg Mountain' in Montana, USA. They date to around 75 million years ago.

▲ *Maiasaura* was a plant-eater about 9 metres long, belonging to the hadrosaur group. Its newly hatched babies were only 40 centimetres long, but within a year they had grown to 150 centimetres.

171 The nest of *Maiasaura* was a mud mound about 2 metres across, with 30–40 eggs and babies. Some fossils show unhatched eggs broken into many small parts, as though squashed by the babies that had already hatched out.

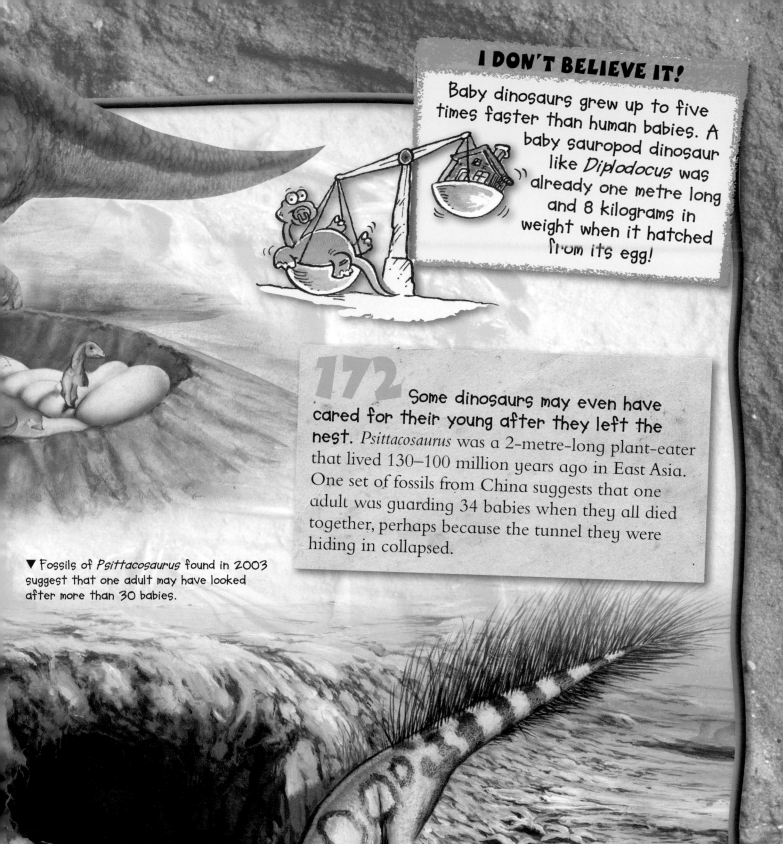

Baby dinosaurs grew up to five times faster than human babies. A baby sauropod dinosaur like *Diplodocus* was already one metre long and 8 kilograms in weight when it hatched from its egg!

172 Some dinosaurs may even have cared for their young after they left the nest. *Psittacosaurus* was a 2-metre-long plant-eater that lived 130–100 million years ago in East Asia. One set of fossils from China suggests that one adult was guarding 34 babies when they all died together, perhaps because the tunnel they were hiding in collapsed.

▼ Fossils of *Psittacosaurus* found in 2003 suggest that one adult may have looked after more than 30 babies.

The end for the dinosaurs

173 About 65 million years ago, the Age of Dinosaurs came to a sudden end. Fossils preserved in the rocks show great changes at this time. However the fossils also show that creatures like fish, insects, birds and mammals carried on. What happened to kill off some of the biggest, most successful animals the world has ever seen? There are many ideas. It could have been one disaster, or a combination of several.

174 The disaster may have been caused by a giant lump of rock, an asteroid or meteorite. This came from outer space and smashed into the Earth. The impact threw up vast clouds of water, rocks, ash and dust that blotted out the Sun for many years. Plants could not grow in the gloom, so many plant-eating dinosaurs died. This meant meat-eaters had less food, so they died as well.

175 Many volcanoes around the Earth could have erupted all at the same time, perhaps due to the meteorite impact. They threw out red-hot rocks, ash, dust and poison gas. Creatures would have choked and died in the gloom.

▼ Scientific studies show that 65.5 million years ago, a space rock smashed into Earth near what is now Yucatan, Mexico.

176 The disaster might have involved a terrible disease. Perhaps this gradually spread among certain kinds of animals and killed them off.

METEORITE SMASH!

You will need:

plastic bowl   flour   large pebble   desk lamp

Put the flour in the bowl. This is Earth's surface. Place the desk lamp so it shines over the top of the bowl. This is the Sun. The pebble is the meteorite from space. Drop the pebble into the bowl. See how the tiny bits of flour float in the air like a mist, making the 'Sun' dimmer. A real meteorite smash may have been the beginning of the end for the great dinosaurs.

177 It might be that dinosaur eggs were eaten by a plague of animals. Small, shrew-like mammals were around at the time. They may have eaten the eggs at night as the dinosaurs slept.

What happened next?

178 **Other kinds of animals died out with dinosaurs.** Flying reptiles called pterosaurs, and swimming reptiles called mosasaurs and plesiosaurs, disappeared. Lots of plants died out too. When a group of living things dies out, it is called an extinction. When many groups disappear at the same time, it's known as a mass extinction.

180 Even though many kinds of animals and plants died out 65 million years ago, other groups lived on. Crabs, shellfish, insects, worms, fish, frogs and mammals all survived the mass extinction – and these groups are still alive today.

179 Several groups of reptiles also survived the mass extinction. They include crocodiles and alligators, turtles and tortoises, lizards and snakes. Why some kinds died out in the great disaster, yet other types survived, is one of the main puzzles that experts today are still trying to solve.

Key

1 Coryphodon (browsing mammal)
2 Gastornis (flightless bird)
3 Eobasileus (browsing mammal)
4 Branisella (early monkey)
5 Tremacebus (early monkey)
6 Paraceratherium (browsing mammal)
7 Arsinoitherium (browsing mammal)

8 Hyracotherium (early horse)
9 Andrewsarchus (carnivorous mammal)
10 Eobasileus (browsing mammal)
11 Plesiadapis (early primate)
12 Ptilodus (squirrel-like mammal)
13 Chriacus (raccoon-like mammal)

181 After the mass extinction, a different group of animals began to take over the land. These were the mammals. Through the Age of Dinosaurs they were mostly small and skulking, coming out only after dark. Now they could change or evolve to become bigger. Within a few million years they had developed into many kinds, from peaceful plant-eaters to huge, fierce predators.

▼ The mass extinction of 65 million years ago killed big dinosaurs and many other kinds of animals and plants. But plenty of animals survived, especially the mammals.

Myths and mistakes

182 Some popular ideas about dinosaurs are probably not true. For example, they are shown in bright colours such as red, yellow, green and blue. This is guesswork. For dinosaurs and other creatures, there are fossils of skin, and also fossilized feathers, as for *Confuciusornis*. But most, being fossils, have turned to stone, so they do not indicate colour. However a few well-preserved feathers show striped patterns, maybe in red and brown.

Toothless beak

Finger claws on wing

183 For many years, people thought that all dinosaurs were slow and stupid animals. But we cannot be sure. Some dinosaurs were quick and agile. Also some, like *Troodon*, had big brains for their body size. They may have been quite intelligent.

◄ Head-to-head butting, shown here by *Wannanosaurus*, is no longer thought likely.

184 Another idea was that 'bone-headed' dinosaurs (pachycephalosaurs) crashed their heads together. It was thought they did this when fighting for mates or to be leader of the herd, just like rams head-butt today. But their domed skulls would probably slip sideways as they thudded together, causing little damage. Maybe they butted each other in the sides instead.

20-centimetre-long wing feathers for agile flight

Wingspan of 70 centimetres

◄ Studies of fossil feathers from *Confuciusornis*, which lived 130 million years ago in China, suggest its plumage may have been red and black.

Long streamer-like tail feathers may have been on the male only

▼ In the movie *The Dinosaur Project* (2012) explorers find living dinosaurs in Africa's Congo forest. However this is purely fiction.

185 Another idea grew up that early cave people had to fight against dinosaurs and kill them — or the other way around. But they did not. There was a very long gap, more than 60 million years, between dinosaurs such as *Tyrannosaurus* and the earliest people.

186 Some people believe that dinosaurs may survive today in remote, faraway places on Earth, such as thick jungle or ocean islands. But most of the Earth has now been visited and explored, and no dinosaurs have been found alive.

I DON'T BELIEVE IT!

One dinosaur's thumb was put on its nose! When scientists first dug up fossils of *Iguanodon*, they found a horn-shaped bone, which fitted *Iguanodon's* nose. Most scientists now believe that the spike was a thumb claw.

How do we know?

▼ Fossils form best in water, such as when drowned dinosaurs were washed by floods into a lake or sea.

1. After death, the dinosaur sinks to the river bed. Worms, crabs and other scavengers eat its soft body parts.

2. Sediments cover the hard body parts, such as bones and teeth, which gradually turn into solid rock.

187 We know about long-gone dinosaurs mainly from the fossils of their body parts. These took thousands or millions of years to form, usually on the bottoms of lakes, rivers or seas, where sand and mud can quickly cover the parts and begin to preserve them. If the animal died on dry land, its parts were more likely to be eaten or rot away.

188 The body parts most likely to fossilize are the hardest ones, which rot away most slowly after death. These include bones, teeth, horns and claws of dinosaurs and other animals, also plant parts such as bark, seeds and cones.

189 Very rarely, a dinosaur or other living thing was buried soon after it died, then a few of the softer body parts also became fossils. These include bits of skin or the remains of the last meal in its stomach.

▲ Bony lumps in the skin of armoured dinosaurs such as ankylosaurs fossilize well — the softer skin has rotted away.

3. Huge earth movements move, lift and tilt the rock layers so they become dry land.

4. Millions of years later the upper rock layers wear away and the fossil remains are exposed.

190 Not all dinosaur fossils are from the actual bodies of dinosaurs. Some are the signs, traces or remains that they left while alive. These include eggshells, nests, tunnels, footprints, and claw and teeth marks on food.

▲ Dino-dropping fossils come in many shapes and sizes! This scientist is an expert in their study.

QUIZ

Which body parts of a dinosaur were most likely to become fossils? Remember, fossils form from the hardest, toughest bits that last long enough to become buried in the rocks and turned to stone.
a. Skull bone b. Muscle c. Leg bone
d. Scaly skin e. Eye f. Blood
g. Claws h. Teeth

Answer:
a. Skull bone
c. Leg bone g. Claws h. Teeth

191 Dinosaur droppings also formed fossils! They are called coprolites and contain broken bits of food, showing what the dinosaur ate. Some dinosaur droppings are as big as a suitcase!

Digging up dinosaurs

▶ At the excavation site or dig, the first tasks are to make surveys by checking the rock for suitable signs of fossils.

◀ Small bits of rock are scraped away. Workers make notes, draw sketches and take photos to record every stage.

192 **Every year, thousands more dinosaur fossils are discovered.** Most of them are from dinosaurs already known to scientists. But five or ten might be from new kinds of dinosaurs. From the fossils, scientists try to work out what the dinosaur looked like and how it lived, all those millions of years ago.

193 **Most dinosaur fossils are found by hard work.** Fossil experts called palaeontologists study the rocks in a region and decide where fossils are most likely to occur. They spend weeks chipping and digging the rock. They look closely at every tiny piece to see if it is part of a fossil. However some dinosaur fossils are found by luck. People out walking in the countryside come across a fossil tooth or bone by chance.

194 Finding all the fossils of a single dinosaur neatly in position is very rare. Usually only a few fossil parts are found from each dinosaur. These are nearly always jumbled up and broken.

▲ After months or years, the restored or 'rebuilt' fossil is complete – this is the skull of *Allosaurus*.

◄ Brushes remove bits of dust, soil and rock flakes. Fragile fossils may be protected with 'jackets' of glass-fibre or plaster.

195 Dinosaur fossils are studied and rebuilt in palaeontology workrooms. They are cleaned and laid out to see which parts are which. It is like trying to put together a jigsaw with most of the pieces missing. Even those that remain are bent and torn. The fossils are put back together, then soft body parts that did not form fossils, such as skin, are added. Scientists use clues from similar animals alive today, such as crocodiles, to help 'rebuild' the dinosaur.

QUIZ

1. What do we call a scientist that studies fossils?

2. How is a fossil 'dig' recorded?

3. How are fossils packed to protect them?

4. What animals can scientists compare dinosaur fossils with?

Answers:
1. A palaeontologist
2. Notes, sketches and photographs
3. They are put in plaster or glass-fibre
4. Crocodiles

Dinosaurs today

196 The name 'dinosaur' was invented in 1842 by English scientist Richard Owen. He realized that the fossils of some prehistoric creatures were reptiles, but different from any known reptile group. So he made a new group, Dinosauria. Its first three members were *Iguanodon*, *Megalosaurus* and *Hylaeosaurus*, all from fossils found in England.

▲ Fossil *Sinosauropteryx* has long legs and feet, lower left. Its tail arches up and forwards to its skull, upper right.

▲ The dinosaur *Caudipteryx* from China had tiny arms and fanned-out tail feathers.

198 In 1996 fossils of the dinosaur *Sinosauropteryx* showed it had feathers. This slim, fast meat-eater, only one metre long, lived 123 million years ago in China. Its feathers were thin and thread-like, not designed for flying.

197 From the 1850s there was a rush to find hundreds of new dinosaurs in North America. In the 1920s exciting discoveries were made in Central Asia. Today, dinosaur remains are being found all over the world, even in frozen Antarctica. Some of the most amazing fossils in recent years come from Argentina and China.

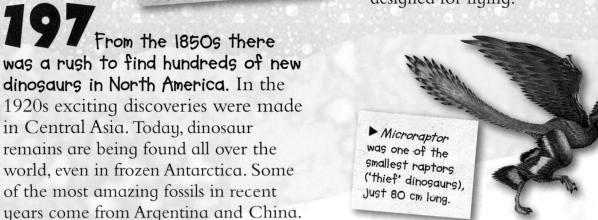

▶ *Microraptor* was one of the smallest raptors ('thief' dinosaurs), just 80 cm long.

▲ *Yutyrannus* was one of the biggest feathered dinosaurs, and weighed almost 2 tonnes. Its fossils are 120 million years old and come from northeast China.

▼ Macaws and other birds are flying dinosaurs of today.

199 Following *Sinosauropteryx*, many more feathered dinosaurs have been found. These include turkey-sized *Caudipteryx*, tiny *Microraptor*, 2-metre *Dilong*, and the huge meat-eater *Yutyrannus*, at over 9 metres in length. But none of these creatures had bodies or feathers designed for flight. However *Archaeopteryx*, which lived 150 million years ago, was a small meat-eater with wide feathers just right for flight.

▶ An early cousin of *Tyrannosaurus*, *Dilong* was also much smaller, about 2 metres from nose to tail.

200 Most experts now believe that birds evolved from small meat-eating dinosaurs. The modern scientific view is that birds are part of the dinosaur group. This means not all dinosaurs died out, or went extinct, 65 million years ago. Some are alive today. They hop, flap and sing in our gardens, parks, wood, seashores and other habitats – they are birds.

I DON'T BELIEVE IT!
The dinosaur with shortest name was also one of the smallest. *Mei* (meaning 'sound asleep') had feathers and was less than 60 centimetres long.

T REX

201 Almost everyone has heard of *Tyrannosaurus rex*. Wasn't it the biggest dinosaur of all time, the greatest meat-eater with a mouth big enough to swallow a car and teeth as long as swords? Not one of these 'facts' is true. Certainly *Tyrannosaurus rex* is one of the world's most famous animals. Even though it died out 65 million years ago, it 'lives on' in movies, toys and games, as statues and works of art, and in music and songs. However, *Tyrannosaurus rex* is also the subject of many mistaken beliefs.

▶ A scene from the 2005 movie *King Kong*. With a mighty roar *Tyrannosaurus rex* bares its huge mouth filled with sharp teeth and prepares to attack. Images like this are familiar — but are they correct? For example, did *T rex* really roar loudly?

Terror of its age

▲ The last dinosaurs of the Late Cretaceous Period ranged from small, speedy hunters such as *Avimimus* to giant plant eaters, three-horned *Triceratops*, spiky *Edmontonia*, hadrosaurs or 'duckbilled' dinosaurs with strange head crests, and of course *T rex*.

KEY
1 Tyrannosaurus rex	5 Parasaurolophus	9 Struthiomimus
2 Triceratops	6 Lambeosaurus	10 Albertosaurus
3 Stegoceras	7 Avimimus	11 Therizinosaurus
4 Edmontonia	8 Corythosaurus	12 Euoplocephalus

202 *T rex*'s full name is *Tyrannosaurus rex*, which means 'king of the tyrant lizards'. However, it wasn't a lizard. It was a large carnivorous or meat-eating animal in the reptile group known as the dinosaurs.

203 Dinosaurs, or 'terrible lizards', lived during a time called the Mesozoic Era (251–65 million years ago). The first dinosaurs appeared about 230 million years ago and all had died out, or become extinct, by 65 million years ago.

204

There were hundreds of kinds of dinosaurs. *Plateosaurus* was a bus-sized herbivore (plant eater) from 210 million years ago. *Brachiosaurus* was a giant herbivore from 150 million years ago. *Deinonychus* was a fierce hunter from about 110 million years ago, and was about the size of an adult human.

205

T rex lived after all of these dinosaurs. Its time was the last part of the Mesozoic Era, known as the Cretaceous Period (145–65 million years ago), from about 68 to 65 million years ago. *T rex* was one of the very last dinosaurs.

ERA	PERIOD	MYA (Million years ago)
MESOZOIC		— 70
		— 80
		— 90
	CRETACEOUS 145.5–65.5 MYA	— 100
		— 110
		— 120
		— 130
		— 140
		— 150
		— 160
	JURASSIC 200–145.5 MYA	— 170
		— 180
		— 190
		— 200
		— 210
		— 220
	TRIASSIC 251–200 MYA	— 230
		— 240
		— 250

Jurassic Period: *Allosaurus* was a big meat-eating dinosaur

Triassic Period: *Herrerasaurus* was one of the first dinosaurs

◄ Dinosaurs ruled the land for 160 million years – longer than any other animal group.

A giant predator

206 The size of fierce animals such as great white sharks, tigers and crocodiles can be exaggerated (made bigger). People often think *T rex* was bigger than it really was.

207 A full-grown *T rex* was over 12 metres long and more than 3 metres high at the hips. It could rear up and raise its head to more than 5 metres above the ground.

▼ *Tyrannosaurus rex* may have been big, but it was smaller than all the other creatures shown here.

Brachiosaurus
13 metres tall
25 metres nose to tail
40-plus tonnes in weight

208 *Tyrannosaurus rex* was not such a giant compared to some plant-eating animals. It was about the same weight as today's African bush elephant, half the size of the extinct imperial mammoth, and one-tenth as heavy as some of the biggest plant-eating dinosaurs.

Imperial mammoth
4.5 metres tall
12 metres nose to tail
10 tonnes in weight

T rex
3–4 metres tall
11–12 metres nose to tail
5 tonnes in weight

Sperm whale
20 metres nose to tail
50 tonnes in weight

209

Compared to today's biggest meat-eating land animals, *Tyrannosaurus rex* was huge. The largest land carnivores today are polar and grizzly bears, up to 3 metres tall and over 600 kilograms. However that's only one-tenth of the weight of *T rex*.

210

Compared to other extinct meat eaters, *Tyrannosaurus rex* was large. The wolf-like *Andrewsarchus* from 40 million years ago was one of the biggest mammal land carnivores. It stood 2 metres tall, was 4 metres long from nose to tail, and weighed more than one tonne.

211

T rex is sometimes called 'the biggest predator of all time'. However it was only one-tenth the size of the sperm whale living in today's oceans, which hunts giant squid. It was also smaller than prehistoric ocean predators such as pliosaurs *Liopleurodon* and *Kronosaurus* (10 tonnes or more) and the ichthyosaur *Shonisaurus* (more than 20 tonnes).

COMPARE HUGE HUNTERS

You will need:
pens   large sheet of paper   animal books

In books or on the Internet, find side-on pictures of *T rex*, a sperm whale, a killer whale and *Andrewsarchus*. Draw them on one sheet of paper to see how they compare:
Sperm whale as long as the paper
T rex nose to tail two-thirds as long as the sperm whale
Killer whale half as long as the sperm whale
Andrewsarchus one-fifth as long as the sperm whale

Profile of T rex

212 Fossil experts can work out what an extinct animal such a *Tyrannosaurus rex* looked like when it was alive. They study the size, shape, length, thickness and other details of its fossil bones, teeth, claws and other parts.

213 The tail of *T rex* was almost half its total length. It had a wide, muscular base and was thick and strong almost to the tip, quite unlike the long, thin, whip-like tails of other dinosaurs such as *Diplodocus*.

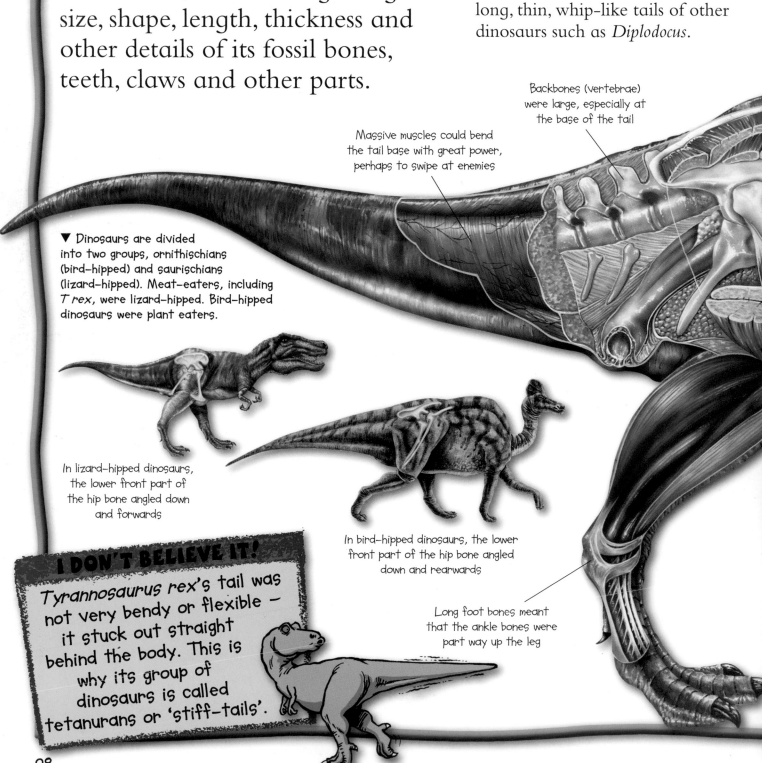

Backbones (vertebrae) were large, especially at the base of the tail

Massive muscles could bend the tail base with great power, perhaps to swipe at enemies

▼ Dinosaurs are divided into two groups, ornithischians (bird-hipped) and saurischians (lizard-hipped). Meat-eaters, including *T rex*, were lizard-hipped. Bird-hipped dinosaurs were plant eaters.

In lizard-hipped dinosaurs, the lower front part of the hip bone angled down and forwards

In bird-hipped dinosaurs, the lower front part of the hip bone angled down and rearwards

Long foot bones meant that the ankle bones were part way up the leg

I DON'T BELIEVE IT!

Tyrannosaurus rex's tail was not very bendy or flexible — it stuck out straight behind the body. This is why its group of dinosaurs is called tetanurans or 'stiff-tails'.

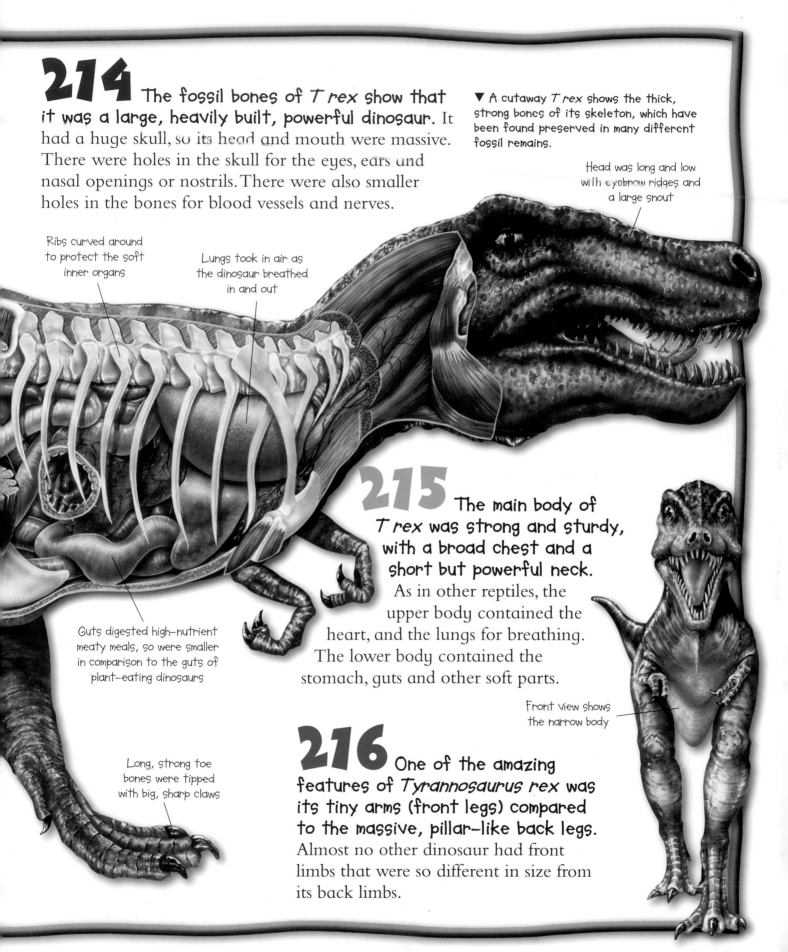

214 The fossil bones of *T rex* show that it was a large, heavily built, powerful dinosaur. It had a huge skull, so its head and mouth were massive. There were holes in the skull for the eyes, ears and nasal openings or nostrils. There were also smaller holes in the bones for blood vessels and nerves.

▼ A cutaway *T rex* shows the thick, strong bones of its skeleton, which have been found preserved in many different fossil remains.

Head was long and low with eyebrow ridges and a large snout

Ribs curved around to protect the soft inner organs

Lungs took in air as the dinosaur breathed in and out

215 The main body of *T rex* was strong and sturdy, with a broad chest and a short but powerful neck. As in other reptiles, the upper body contained the heart, and the lungs for breathing. The lower body contained the stomach, guts and other soft parts.

Guts digested high-nutrient meaty meals, so were smaller in comparison to the guts of plant-eating dinosaurs

Front view shows the narrow body

Long, strong toe bones were tipped with big, sharp claws

216 One of the amazing features of *Tyrannosaurus rex* was its tiny arms (front legs) compared to the massive, pillar-like back legs. Almost no other dinosaur had front limbs that were so different in size from its back limbs.

Was T rex clever?

▼ Many dinosaurs had eyes on the sides of the head, giving good all-round vision but not a detailed front view. T rex had forward-facing eyes.

View from forward-facing eyes

View from sideways-facing eyes

▶ T rex probably used its long tongue to lick and taste meat before it started to eat.

217 The skull of T rex is well known from several good fossils. They show that the large eyes were set at an angle so they looked forwards rather than to the sides. This allowed T rex to see an object in front with both eyes and judge its distance well.

218 As far as we know dinosaurs, like other reptiles, lacked ear flaps. Instead they had eardrums of thin skin on the sides of their heads so they could hear.

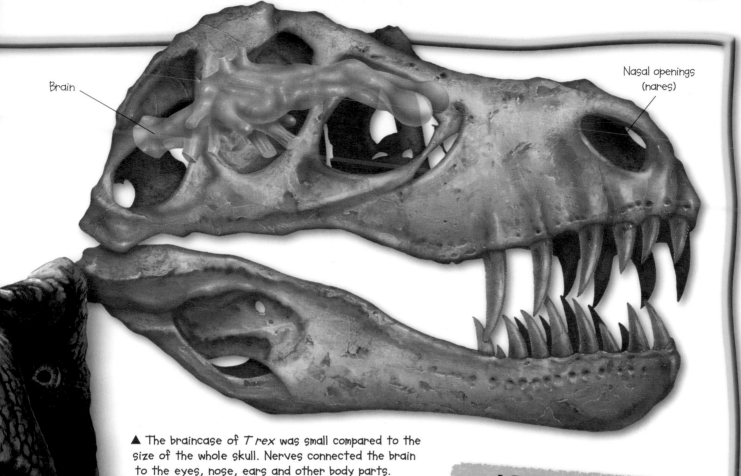

Brain

Nasal openings (nares)

▲ The braincase of *T rex* was small compared to the size of the whole skull. Nerves connected the brain to the eyes, nose, ears and other body parts.

219
T rex's big nasal openings were at the top of its snout. They opened into a very large chamber inside the skull, which detected smells floating in the air. *T rex*'s sense of smell, like its eyesight, was very good.

I DON'T BELIEVE IT!
The eyeballs of *Tyrannosaurus rex* were up to 8 centimetres across – but those of today's giant squid are almost 30 centimetres!

220
Some fossils even show the size and shape of *T rex*'s brain! The brain was in a casing called the cranium in the upper rear of the skull. This can be seen in well-preserved skulls. The space inside shows the brain's shape.

221
Tyrannosaurus rex had the biggest brain of almost any dinosaur. The parts dealing with the sense of smell, called the olfactory lobes, were especially large. So *T rex* had keen senses of sight, hearing and especially smell. And it wasn't stupid.

What big teeth!

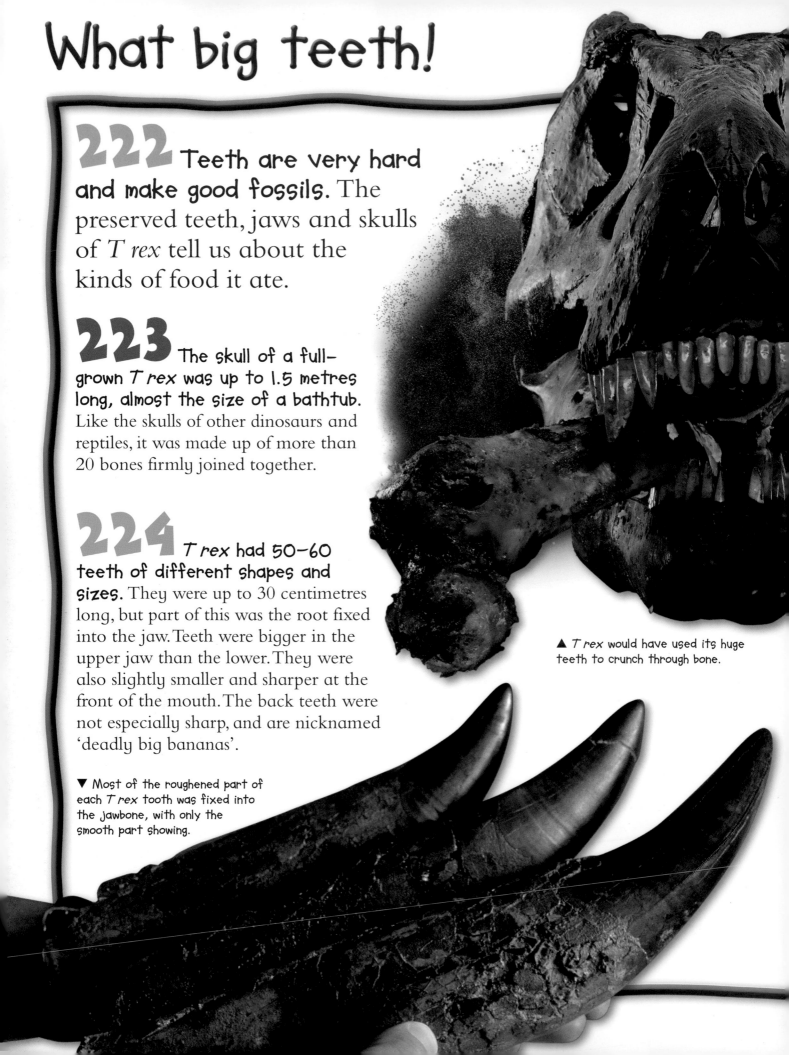

222 Teeth are very hard and make good fossils. The preserved teeth, jaws and skulls of *T rex* tell us about the kinds of food it ate.

223 The skull of a full-grown *T rex* was up to 1.5 metres long, almost the size of a bathtub. Like the skulls of other dinosaurs and reptiles, it was made up of more than 20 bones firmly joined together.

224 *T rex* had 50–60 teeth of different shapes and sizes. They were up to 30 centimetres long, but part of this was the root fixed into the jaw. Teeth were bigger in the upper jaw than the lower. They were also slightly smaller and sharper at the front of the mouth. The back teeth were not especially sharp, and are nicknamed 'deadly big bananas'.

▼ Most of the roughened part of each *T rex* tooth was fixed into the jawbone, with only the smooth part showing.

▲ *T rex* would have used its huge teeth to crunch through bone.

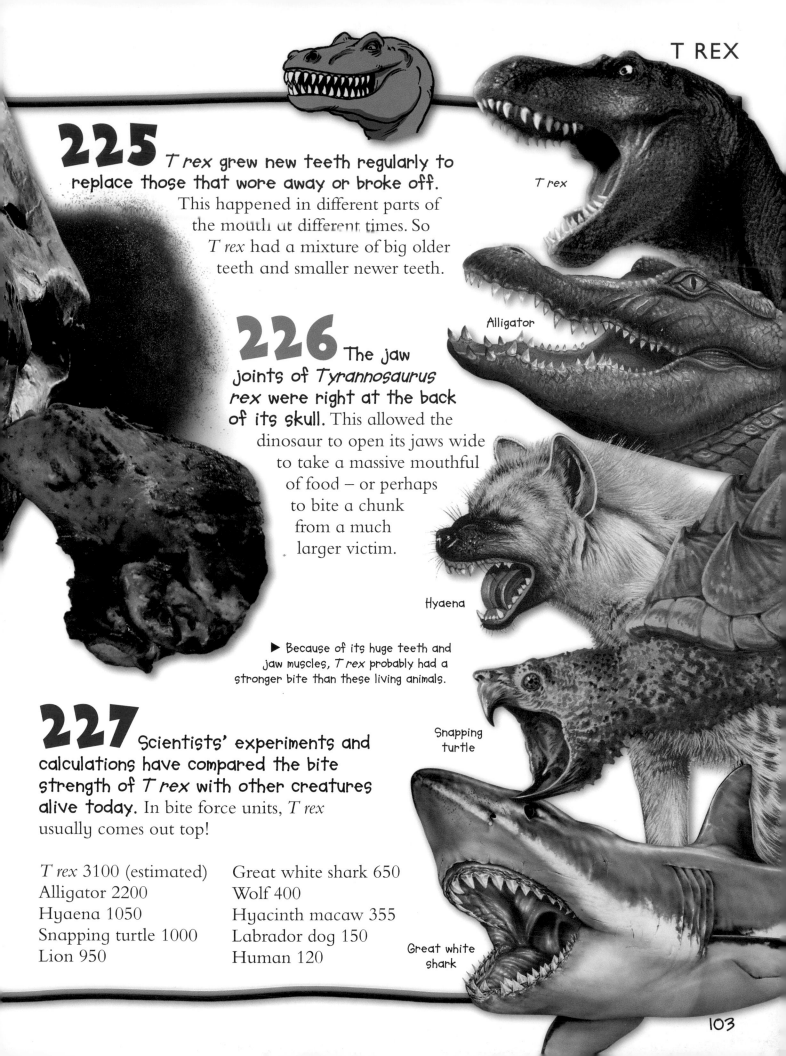

225

T rex grew new teeth regularly to replace those that wore away or broke off. This happened in different parts of the mouth at different times. So *T rex* had a mixture of big older teeth and smaller newer teeth.

T rex

226

The jaw joints of *Tyrannosaurus rex* were right at the back of its skull. This allowed the dinosaur to open its jaws wide to take a massive mouthful of food – or perhaps to bite a chunk from a much larger victim.

Alligator

Hyaena

▶ Because of its huge teeth and jaw muscles, *T rex* probably had a stronger bite than these living animals.

Snapping turtle

227

Scientists' experiments and calculations have compared the bite strength of *T rex* with other creatures alive today. In bite force units, *T rex* usually comes out top!

T rex 3100 (estimated)
Alligator 2200
Hyaena 1050
Snapping turtle 1000
Lion 950

Great white shark 650
Wolf 400
Hyacinth macaw 355
Labrador dog 150
Human 120

Great white shark

Tiny arms, big legs

228 **Tyrannosaurus rex's strangest features were its tiny arms.** In fact, they were about the same size as the arms of an adult human, even though *T rex* was more than 50 times bigger than a person. Yet the arms were not weak. They had powerful muscles and two strong clawed fingers.

▶ *T rex*'s arms were so small, they could not even be used for passing food to the mouth.

229 **What did *Tyrannosaurus rex* use its mini-arms for?** There have been many suggestions such as holding onto a victim while biting, pushing itself off the ground if it fell over, and holding onto a partner at breeding time. Perhaps we will never know the true reason.

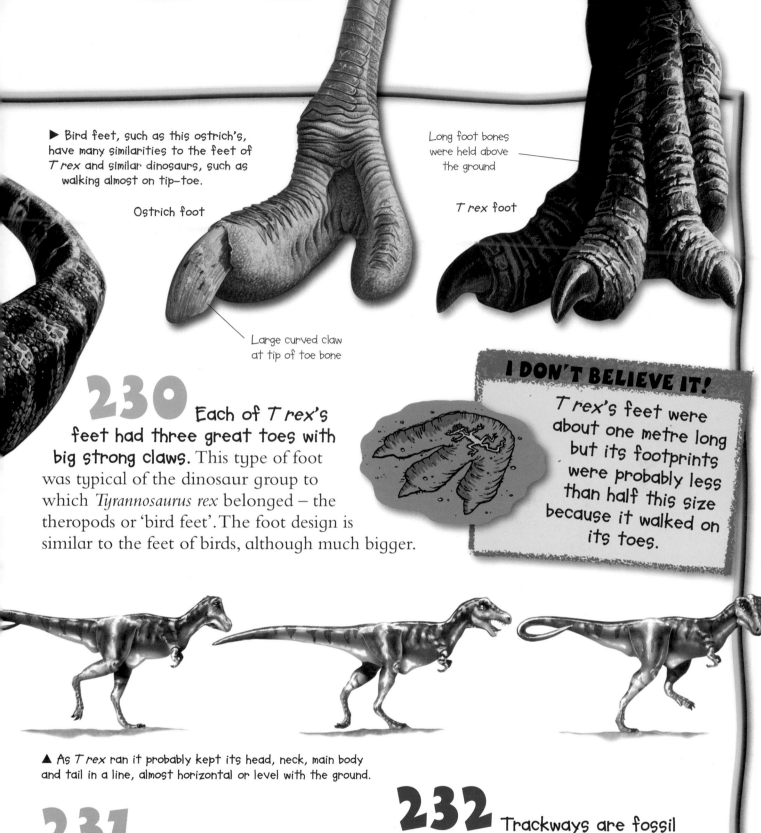

▶ Bird feet, such as this ostrich's, have many similarities to the feet of *T rex* and similar dinosaurs, such as walking almost on tip-toe.

Ostrich foot

Long foot bones were held above the ground

T rex foot

Large curved claw at tip of toe bone

230
Each of *T rex*'s feet had three great toes with big strong claws. This type of foot was typical of the dinosaur group to which *Tyrannosaurus rex* belonged – the theropods or 'bird feet'. The foot design is similar to the feet of birds, although much bigger.

I DON'T BELIEVE IT!
T rex's feet were about one metre long but its footprints were probably less than half this size because it walked on its toes.

▲ As *T rex* ran it probably kept its head, neck, main body and tail in a line, almost horizontal or level with the ground.

231
The big, heavy back legs of *Tyrannosaurus rex* show that the dinosaur could make long strides as it walked and ran. The three parts of the leg – the thigh, shin and foot – were all about the same length.

232
Trackways are fossil footprints in mud and sand that give clues to how an animal moved. There are some trackways that could have been made by *Tyrannosaurus rex* or similar dinosaurs. They help to show how fast it walked and ran.

What did T rex eat?

233 *Tyrannosaurus rex* was a huge hunter, so it probably ate big prey. Other large dinosaurs of its time and place were plant eaters. They included three-horned *Triceratops* and its cousins, and various 'duckbilled' dinosaurs (hadrosaurs) such as *Parasaurolophus* and *Edmontosaurus*.

▼ The giant pterosaur (flying reptile) *Quetzalcoatlus* lived at about the same time as *T rex*. It may have pecked at the remains of a *T rex* kill after the dinosaur had finished feasting.

234 *T rex* could have used its huge mouth, strong teeth and powerful jaw muscles to attack these big plant eaters. It may have lunged at a victim with one massive bite to cause a slashing wound. Then it would retreat a short distance and wait for the prey to weaken from blood loss before moving in to feed.

◄ An adult *Triceratops* would be a fierce foe for *T rex* to tackle. However young, sick and old *Triceratops* might have been easier to kill.

235 One fossil of *Triceratops* has scratch-like gouge marks on its large, bony neck frill. These could have been made by *Tyrannosaurus rex* teeth. The marks are about the correct distance apart, matching the spacing of *T rex* teeth.

► The hadrosaur *Parasaurolophus* might have made loud trumpeting noises through its hollow tube-like head crest, to warn others in its herd that *T rex* was near.

▶ Coprolites can be broken apart or sawn through to study the bits of bones, teeth and other items inside.

236 Coprolites are preserved lumps of animal dung or droppings, fossilized into hard stone. Several large coprolites have been found that could be from *Tyrannosaurus rex*. They show many jumbled fragments of bone from its victims, including young *Edmontosaurus* and *Triceratops*.

237 In some dinosaurs, several fossil skeletons have been found preserved together, suggesting they lived as a pack or herd. The remains of several *Tyrannosaurus rex* have also been found in this way, which might suggest a family or a pack-hunting group. Some experts say that more evidence is needed for this idea.

▶ Armoured dinosaurs like *Euoplocephalus* may have defended themselves against *T rex* by swinging their heavy, clubbed tails.

Hunter or scavenger?

238 Was *T rex* an active hunter that chased after its victims? Was it an ambush predator that hid in wait to rush out at prey? Was it a scavenger that ate any dead or dying dinosaurs it found? Or did it chase other dinosaurs from their kills and steal the meal for itself?

239 To be an active pursuit hunter, *T rex* must have been able to run fast. Scientists have tried to work out its running speed using models and computers, and by comparisons with other animals.

WHO DOES WHAT?

Research these animals living today and find out if they are mainly fast hunters, sneaky ambushers or scavengers.
Tiger Cheetah Hyaena
Crocodile Vulture
African wild dog

▶ *Tyrannosaurus rex* may have run down smaller dinosaurs such as these *Prenocephale*, perhaps rushing out from its hiding place in a clump of trees.

▲ When scavenging, *T rex* might sniff out a dinosaur that had died from illness or injury.

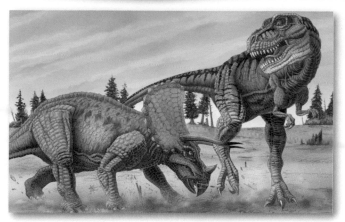

▲ When hunting, *T rex* would be at risk from injury, such as from the horns of *Triceratops*.

240 Some estimates for the running speed of *T rex* are as fast as 50 kilometres an hour, others as slow as 15 kilometres an hour. Most give a speed of between 20 and 30 kilometres an hour. This is slightly slower than a human sprinter, but probably faster than typical *T rex* prey such as *Triceratops*.

241 Evidence that *T rex* was a scavenger includes its very well developed sense of smell for sniffing out dead, rotting bodies. Also, its powerful teeth could not chew food repeatedly like we do, but they could crush bones at first bite to get at the nutritious jelly-like marrow inside. Maybe a hungry *Tyrannosaurus rex* simply ate anything it could catch or find, so it was a hunter, ambusher and scavenger all in one.

242 Several *T rex* fossils show injuries to body parts such as shins, ribs, neck and jaws. These could have been made by victims fighting back, suggesting that *T rex* hunted live prey.

▶ *T rex* would tear and rip flesh from large prey, gulp in lumps and swallow them whole.

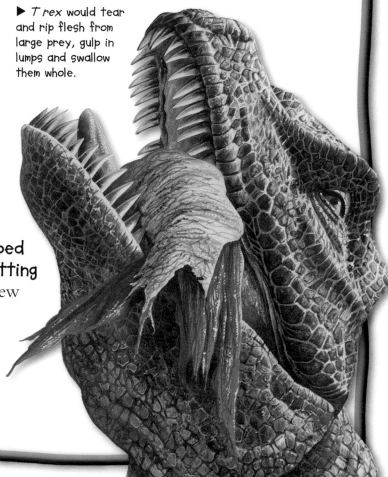

Growing up

243 Did *T rex* live in groups? Most of its fossils are of lone individuals. Some were found near other specimens of *T rex*. These could have been preserved near each other by chance, or they could have been a group that all died together.

Embryo   Yolk

▲ A baby dinosaur developed as an embryo in its egg, fed by nutrients from the yolk.

▶ The baby probably hatched out by biting through the tough shell, which was flexible like leather.

244 Living reptiles lay eggs that hatch into young, and dinosaurs such as *T rex* probably did the same. Many fossil dinosaur eggs have been discovered, but none are known for certain to be from *T rex*. Some dinosaurs laid eggs in nests and looked after their young, but again there are no fossils like this for *T rex*.

246 It seems that *T rex* grew slowly for about 12–14 years. Then suddenly it grew very fast, putting on about 2 kilograms every day as a teenager. By 20 years it was full-grown.

▶ Young *T rex* may have killed small prey such as birds, lizards and newly hatched dinosaurs.

245 Fossils of individual *T rex* are of different sizes and ages, showing how this dinosaur grew up. Some of the fossil bones are so well preserved that they have 'growth rings' almost like a tree trunk, showing growth speed.

247 Can we tell apart female and male *Tyrannosaurus rex* from their fossils? Some scientists thought that females were bigger, with stronger, thicker bones than the males. However the latest evidence makes this less clear.

▶ In many reptiles today, the adults keep growing with age. However their growth rate gradually reduces, so they get bigger more slowly. It is not certain if dinosaurs such as *T rex* grew like this.

248 The biggest *T rex* found, 'Sue', was about 28 years old when it died. No one knows for certain if *Tyrannosaurus rex* could live longer. As with many of these questions, more fossil finds will help to fill in the details.

Where in the world?

249 T rex was one kind, or species, of dinosaur in a group of species known as the genus *Tyrannosaurus*. Were there any other members of this genus?

250 After T rex fossils were discovered and named over 100 years ago, fossil-hunters began to find the remains of many similar huge predators. Some were given their own names in the genus *Tyrannosaurus*, but most have now been renamed *Tyrannosaurus rex*.

251 *Tarbosaurus*, 'terrifying lizard', was very similar to T rex, almost as big, and it lived at the same time. However its fossils come from Asia – Mongolia and China – rather than North America. Some experts consider it to be another species of *Tyrannosaurus*, called *Tyrannosaurus bataar*. Others think that it's so similar to T rex that it should be called *Tyrannosaurus rex*.

252 Fossils of smaller dinosaurs similar to T rex have been found in Europe. They include 6-metre-long *Eotyrannus*, from more than 100 million years ago, from the Isle of Wight, southern England. Fossils of *Aviatyrannis* from Portugal are even older, from the Jurassic Period.

◀ *Tarbosaurus* had big teeth, tiny arms and many other features similar to T rex. It was named by Russian fossil expert Evgeny Maleev in 1955, exactly 50 years after T rex was named.

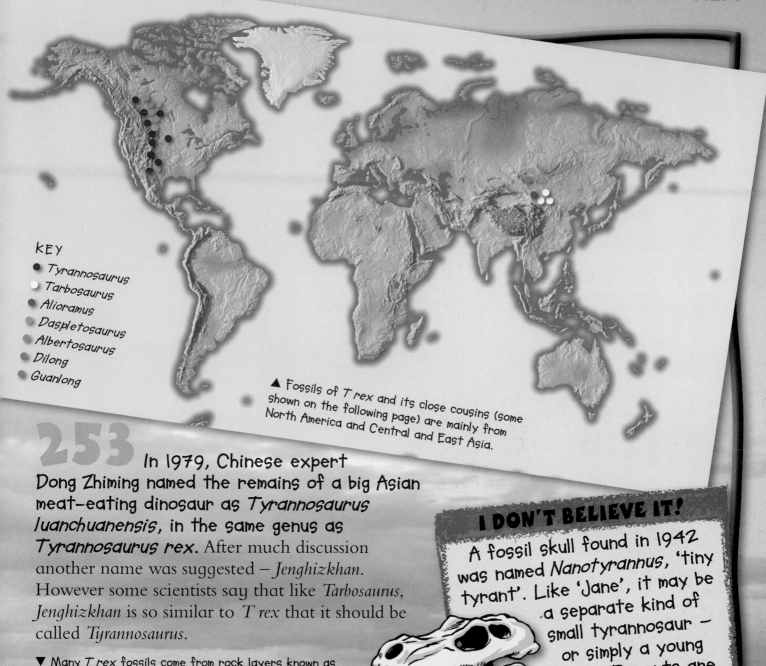

KEY
- Tyrannosaurus
- Tarbosaurus
- Alioramus
- Daspletosaurus
- Albertosaurus
- Dilong
- Guanlong

▲ Fossils of *T rex* and its close cousins (some shown on the following page) are mainly from North America and Central and East Asia.

253 In 1979, Chinese expert Dong Zhiming named the remains of a big Asian meat-eating dinosaur as *Tyrannosaurus luanchuanensis*, in the same genus as *Tyrannosaurus rex*. After much discussion another name was suggested – *Jenghizkhan*. However some scientists say that like *Tarbosaurus*, *Jenghizkhan* is so similar to *T rex* that it should be called *Tyrannosaurus*.

▼ Many *T rex* fossils come from rock layers known as the Hell Creek Formation. These are found mainly in Montana, also in parts of Wyoming, North Dakota and South Dakota, USA.

I DON'T BELIEVE IT!

A fossil skull found in 1942 was named *Nanotyrannus*, 'tiny tyrant'. Like 'Jane', it may be a separate kind of small tyrannosaur – or simply a young *T rex*. Experts are undecided.

Tyrannosaur group

254 **What kind of dinosaur was *Tyrannosaurus rex*?** It belonged to the group called tyrannosaurs, known scientifically as the family *Tyrannosauridae*. These dinosaurs had bones, joints and other features that were different from other predatory dinosaurs. They were part of an even bigger group, the tyrannosauroids.

Tyrannosaurus rex

Nanotyrannus (could be same as Tyrannosaurus)

Tarbosaurus (could be same as Tyrannosaurus)

Tyrannosaurine subfamily

▲ *Guanlong* may have shown off the crest of thin bone on its head to possible partners at breeding time.

255 **One of the first tyrannosauroids was *Guanlong*, or 'crown dragon'.** Its fossils were discovered in China in 2006 and are about 160 million years old – nearly 100 million years before *Tyrannosaurus rex*. It was 3 metres long and had a strange horn-like plate of bone on its nose.

▼ The 'feathers' of *Dilong* were similar to fur and may have kept its body warm.

256 **Another early cousin of *T rex* was *Dilong*, 'emperor dragon', also from China.** Its fossils date to 130 million years ago. *Dilong* was about 2 metres long when fully grown. It had traces of hair-like feathers on the head and tail. As shown later, some experts suggest *Tyrannosaurus rex* itself may have had some kind of feathers.

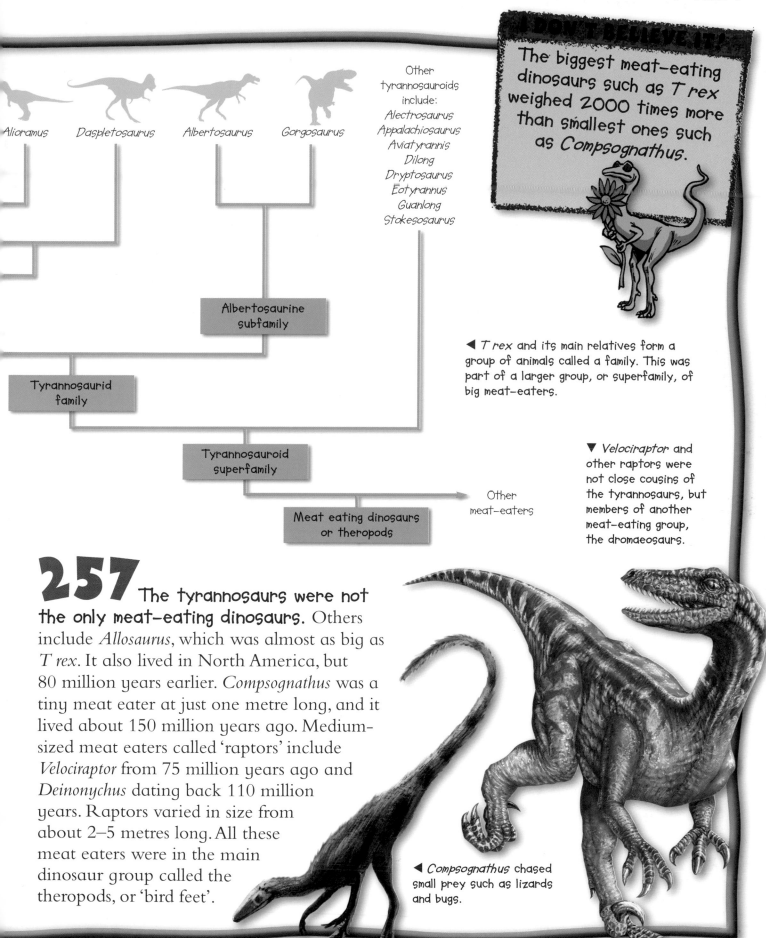

Alioramus   Daspletosaurus   Albertosaurus   Gorgosaurus

Other
tyrannosauroids
include:
Alectrosaurus
Appalachiosaurus
Aviatyrannis
Dilong
Dryptosaurus
Eotyrannus
Guanlong
Stokesosaurus

Albertosaurine
subfamily

Tyrannosaurid
family

Tyrannosauroid
superfamily

Meat eating dinosaurs
or theropods

Other
meat-eaters

I DON'T BELIEVE IT!

The biggest meat-eating dinosaurs such as T rex weighed 2000 times more than smallest ones such as Compsognathus.

◀ T rex and its main relatives form a group of animals called a family. This was part of a larger group, or superfamily, of big meat-eaters.

▼ Velociraptor and other raptors were not close cousins of the tyrannosaurs, but members of another meat-eating group, the dromaeosaurs.

257 The tyrannosaurs were not the only meat-eating dinosaurs. Others include *Allosaurus*, which was almost as big as *T rex*. It also lived in North America, but 80 million years earlier. *Compsognathus* was a tiny meat eater at just one metre long, and it lived about 150 million years ago. Medium-sized meat eaters called 'raptors' include *Velociraptor* from 75 million years ago and *Deinonychus* dating back 110 million years. Raptors varied in size from about 2–5 metres long. All these meat eaters were in the main dinosaur group called the theropods, or 'bird feet'.

◀ Compsognathus chased small prey such as lizards and bugs.

Close cousins

258 In the tyrannosaur group with *T rex* were several of its closest relatives. They were big, fierce dinosaurs, but most lived before *T rex* and were not quite as large.

▲ There are many fossil remains of *Gorgosaurus*, making it one of the best known of all the tyrannosaurs. It had a small horn-like crest above each eye.

259 Fossils of *Gorgosaurus*, 'fierce lizard', come mainly from Alberta, Canada and are 75–70 million years old. *Gorgosaurus* was very similar to *Albertosaurus*, although slightly smaller at 8–9 metres long. Like all tyrannosaurs, it had hollow bones and openings in its skull that helped to reduce its weight. Some experts think that *Gorgosaurus* was really a kind of *Albertosaurus* and that its name should be changed.

260 *Daspletosaurus*, 'frightful lizard', was another dinosaur from Alberta, 80–75 million years ago. Its fossils are also known from other regions of North America, as far south as New Mexico, USA. It was about 8 metres long with especially large jaws and teeth. Its arms were small, but not quite so tiny compared to its body as those of *Tyrannosaurus rex*.

▲ *Daspletosaurus* weighed about 2.5 tonnes and had a skull more than one metre long.

▼ *Alectrosaurus* from Mongolia, Asia was one of the smaller tyrannosaurs, some 5 metres in total length.

▶ *Appalachiosaurus* fossils come from Alabama, USA, which is an area where few other tyrannosaurs have been found. Only one 7-metre-long skeleton has been found, but it was probably not fully grown.

261 *Albertosaurus*, 'Alberta lizard', dates from about 75–70 million years ago. Its fossils were first found in Alberta, Canada. It looked similar to *T rex*, with a huge mouth and sharp teeth, small arms and powerful legs, but it was smaller, at 9–10 metres and around 1.5 tonnes. At one site the remains of over 20 *Albertosaurus* were found, from adults to teenagers to youngsters. This could have been a mixed pack out hunting.

Working with fossils

▼ There are several stages to the fossilization process, which can take many millions of years.

1. A dinosaur dies and falls into a lake or river, where it sinks to the bottom. The flesh and other soft body parts rot away or are eaten by water-dwelling creatures.

2. The bones and teeth are buried under layers of mud and sand. Silica and other minerals from the rock seep into the bones, filling any available gaps.

3. Over a period of millions of years, minerals replace the original dinosaur bones entirely, but preserve their shape and form. The bones have become fossils.

4. If the rock containing the fossils is pushed up and eroded (worn away) the fossils become exposed. They may then be discovered by a scientist so they can be excavated.

267 Like all animal fossils, those of *T rex* are of the harder parts of the body. They have been preserved in rocks and, over many millions of years, gradually turned to stone.

268 For dinosaurs, the body parts that form fossils are mainly bones, teeth, claws, horns, and less often, skin. There are also fossilized eggs, footprints or trackways, coprolites (droppings) and other clues.

269 Like many other prehistoric creatures, most *T rex* fossils are broken scraps, squashed bits and crushed pieces. They are often very difficult to put together, and scientists have trouble identifying the original animals.

I DON'T BELIEVE IT!

Some *T rex* fossils show injuries that may have been caused by the teeth of other *T rex*. Perhaps they were fighting over food, territory, or breeding partners, or who was boss.

▶ *Archaeopteryx*, the earliest known bird, lived about 80 million years before *T rex*. Its bones show many similarities to small meat-eating dinosaurs.

270 Reptiles today are cold-blooded, but were *T rex* and some other dinosaurs warm-blooded, like mammals and birds? Fossils show that *T rex*'s bone structure and growth rate were similar to mammals and birds. There is also evidence that the chemical make-up of its preserved bones resembles birds. But there is no complete proof one way or the other.

▶ A palaeontologist working at a *T rex* dig site. A variety of tools and special equipment is needed to help remove the fossils from the ground.

271 In 2008, 68-million-year-old fossils of *T rex* (named 'B rex' by palaeontologists) were unearthed in Montana, USA. Examining these very well-preserved bones with a microscope showed they were similar to those of living female birds. So 'B rex' may well have been a female *T rex* producing eggs inside her body when she died aged 15–20 years.

Rebuilding T rex

272 Fossil experts use preserved bones and other parts of T rex to show what it looked like when alive. The bones are also compared to those of similar animals alive today, known as comparative anatomy. For T rex, similar living animals include crocodiles, lizards – and birds.

273 Some fossil bones have patches, grooves and ridges called 'muscle scars'. They show where the animal's muscles were joined to the bones in life. This helps experts to work out how the muscles pulled the bones and how T rex moved when it was alive.

274 As with other extinct creatures, there are no remains of T rex's soft body parts such as the stomach, guts, heart and lungs. These were eaten by scavengers soon after death or were rotted away. However experts can use comparative anatomy with living creatures to imagine what T rex's soft body parts looked like.

▼ Fossil dinosaur skin has a scaly surface, similar to many of today's reptiles.

275 Skin and scales of dinosaurs sometimes form fossils. However they are the colour of the rocks that make the fossils, not the colour of the original skin and scales. So we have no way of knowing T rex's true colour in life.

◀ Close cousins of T rex have been preserved with simple hair-like feathers on their skin. It may be possible that T rex also had feathers.

▲ This reconstruction of *T rex* shows the modern idea of its body position, with tail held straight out behind, When the skull is moved from the trolley to the front end of the neck bones, it will be positioned low, not high as previously thought.

▶ For many years, *T rex* was thought to hold its head up high and drag its tail along the ground.

276 The first reconstructions of *T rex* showed it standing almost upright like a kangaroo. However from its bone and joint shapes, most experts now think that it held its head and body level with the ground, balanced over its big back legs by its long, heavy tail.

The story of Sue

277 The biggest *Tyrannosaurus rex* found so far is 'Sue'. Its official code number is FMNH PR2081, from the Field Museum of Natural History in Chicago, USA.

278 'Sue' is named after its discoverer, Sue Hendrickson. She was working at a fossil dig in 1990 near the town of Faith, in South Dakota, USA, when she uncovered parts of a massive *T rex*. An entire team of people helped to dig up and clean the remains.

279 'Sue' is amazingly complete for a fossil animal, with about four-fifths of its teeth, bones and other parts preserved. The dinosaur was probably covered with mud soon after it died, which prevented scavenging animals from cracking open or carrying away its bones.

280 'Sue' dates from between 67 and 65.5 million years ago. It measures 12.8 metres from nose to tail-tip and 4 metres tall at the hips. The weight of 'Sue' when alive was probably between 5.5 and 6.5 tonnes.

◄ Sue Hendrickson with the fossil foot of 'Sue'. As well as finding 'Sue' the *T rex*, Sue Hendrickson is an expert diver and has explored shipwrecks and sunken cities.

◄ In May 2000, 'Sue' went on display at the Field Museum of Chicago and has been the star attraction ever since.

I DON'T BELIEVE IT!
Despite the name 'Sue', it's not clear if this T rex specimen was female or male. But it's a true 'Sue-perstar' with more than a million visitors each year!

281 After 'Sue' was discovered, there was a dispute about who owned the fossils. Various people claimed them, including the landowner, the dig team, the organizers of the excavation and the local authorities. After a legal battle, 'Sue' was sold at auction in 1997 in New York. The Field Museum of Chicago paid $8.39 million.

Stan, Jane and the rest

282 Apart from 'Sue', there are more than 30 other sets of *T rex* fossils. Some are just a few bones and teeth, while others are well preserved, fairly complete skeletons.

283 'Stan' is named after its discoverer Stan Sacrisen. Code numbered BHI 3033, it was dug up near Buffalo, South Dakota, USA in 1992 by a team from the Black Hills Institute. 'Stan' was about 12.2 metres long and 3 tonnes in weight, with 199 bones and 58 teeth. Some bones show signs of injuries that had healed, including broken ribs, a damaged neck and a tooth wound in the skull.

284 'Wankel rex', specimen MOR 555, was found by Kathy Wankel in 1988. It was excavated by a team from the Museum of the Rockies and is now on show at that museum in Bozeman, Montana.

285 'Tinker', also called 'Kid Rex', was a young *Tyrannosaurus rex*. About two-thirds adult size, it was found in 1998 in South Dakota and named after the leader of the fossil-hunting team, Ron 'Tinker' Frithiof.

▶ 'Stan' is now at the Black Hills Museum in Hill City, South Dakota.

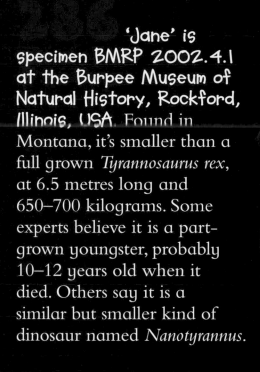

'Jane' is specimen BMRP 2002.4.1 at the Burpee Museum of Natural History, Rockford, Illinois, USA. Found in Montana, it's smaller than a full grown *Tyrannosaurus rex*, at 6.5 metres long and 650–700 kilograms. Some experts believe it is a part-grown youngster, probably 10–12 years old when it died. Others say it is a similar but smaller kind of dinosaur named *Nanotyrannus*.

▶ The fossils of 'Jane' from Montana's Hell Creek took more than four years to dig out, clean up and put together for display.

A NEW NAME FOR T REX

You will need:

pictures of *T rex* in different poses
pen   paper

Copy some pictures of *T rex* onto your paper. Imagine you and your friends have discovered their fossils and given them nicknames. Write these next to your drawings. Perhaps *T rex* should be named after you?

127

Bigger than the 'king'

287 Until the 1990s, *Tyrannosaurus rex* was famous as the biggest predatory land creature of all time. But the past few years have seen discoveries of even bigger meat-eating or carnivorous dinosaurs.

288 Fossils of *Giganotosaurus*, 'southern giant reptile', were uncovered in 1993 in Patagonia, Argentina. This huge hunter was slightly bigger than *T rex*, at more than 13 metres long and weighing over 6 tonnes. *Giganotosaurus* lived earlier than *T rex*, about 95–90 million years ago.

289 Fossils of *Spinosaurus* were first found in Egypt in 1912. This predator lived 100–95 million years ago, and had long, bony rods sticking up from its back that may have held up a 'sail' of skin. The original remains suggested a big predator, but not as big as *T rex*. However recent finds indicate that *Spinosaurus* may have been larger, maybe 16 metres long and 7 tonnes in weight.

QUIZ

Put these dinosaurs in order of size, biggest to smallest:
Tyrannosaurus rex   Deinonychus
Brachiosaurus   Spinosaurus
Compsognathus   Giganotosaurus

Answers:
Brachiosaurus, Spinosaurus,
Giganotosaurus, Tyrannosaurus rex,
Deinonychus, Compsognathus

290 *Carcharodontosaurus*, 'shark tooth lizard', was another massive hunter from North Africa. It was first named in 1931 and lived 100–95 million years ago. Recent discoveries in Morocco and Niger show that it could have been about the same size as *T rex*.

291 Another *T rex*–sized dinosaur was *Mapusaurus*, which lived in Argentina around the same time as *T rex* lived in North America. It was not as heavily built as *T rex*, weighing about 3 tonnes.

▼ This skull of *Carcharodontosaurus* measures more than 1.7 metres in length, with teeth 20 centimetres long. The human skull just in front of it gives an idea of just how big this dinosaur was.

▶ *T rex* and the other meat eaters were not the biggest dinosaurs by far. Much larger are huge plant eaters such as *Brachiosaurus* and *Argentinosaurus*.

T rex superstar

292 *Tyrannosaurus rex* is far more than a big meat-eating dinosaur. It's a world superstar, alongside such famous creatures as the great white shark, blue whale, gorilla, tiger and golden eagle. If *Tyrannosaurus rex* was alive today and could charge money for using its name, pictures, sponsorships and advertising, it would be mega-rich!

293 Ever since its fossils were discovered, *T rex* has starred in books, plays and movies. It's featured in films such as *The Lost World* (first made in 1925, then again in 1960 and 1992), several *King Kong* movies, the animated *The Land Before Time* (1988), and the *Night at the Museum* movies (2006, 2009).

▼ In *Night at the Museum*, Rexy the *T rex* skeleton looks fierce but is really quite cute and chases bones like a puppy.

I DON'T BELIEVE IT!

T rex was one of the stars of the *Jurassic Park* movies. However it didn't live in the Jurassic Period, it lived 80 million years later at the end of the Cretaceous Period.

Gems & Min

▶ In *T rex: Back to the Cretaceous* (1998), Ally finds a mysterious egg–like rock — which transports her back to the end of the Dinosaur Age.

294
In movies, *Tyrannosaurus rex* is perhaps most famous from the *Jurassic Park* series. These began with *Jurassic Park* itself in 1993, then *The Lost World: Jurassic Park* in 1997, and *Jurassic Park 3* in 2001. *Tyrannosaurus rex is* shown breaking out of its fenced enclosure, attacking people and generally causing havoc – but also looking after and protecting its baby with great care.

295
Toy Story movies, games and other products feature an unusual *Tyrannosaurus rex* toy called 'Rex' who is nervous, weedy and worried. This is very unlike the usual fearsome character given to *T rex*.

▶ The *T rex* of *Jurassic Park* tries to sniff out human prey, but in the end it saves them from being attacked by marauding raptor dinosaurs.

What next for T rex?

296 Why did *T rex* die out 65 million years ago, along with all other dinosaurs? The main suggestion is that a huge lump of rock from space, an asteroid, hit Earth and caused worldwide disasters of giant waves, volcanic eruptions and a dust cloud that blotted out the Sun. In this end-of Cretaceous mass extinction no dinosaurs, not even the great *T rex*, could survive.

▶ A dinosaur fan comes face to face with *T rex* at the *Walking with Dinosaurs* tour, 2009. Animatronic (mechanical model) dinosaurs move and roar, but unlike the real ones, they are harmless.

297 Our ideas about *T rex* do not stand still. As scientists discover more fossils and invent new methods of studying them, we learn more about *T rex* and the other animals and plants of its time.

298 Could *Tyrannosaurus rex* or similar dinosaurs still survive today, in thick jungle or on remote mountains? Most of the world's land has now been explored or photographed from aircraft and satellites. Sadly, there's no sign of *T rex* or other big unknown animals.

299 Could *T rex* somehow be brought back to life from its fossil remains? Even with the latest scientific methods, this is still a very remote and faraway possibility. Even if it worked, where would *Tyrannosaurus rex* live and what would it eat? Its habitat, with the climate, scenery, plants and animals, is long gone.

300 *Tyrannosaurus rex* no longer holds the record as the biggest land predator of all time. But it's such a well known celebrity around the world that it will probably remain the most famous dinosaur, and one of the most popular creatures of all, for many years to come.

FOSSILS

301 Without fossils, we would know nothing about prehistoric life. Fossils are the remains of animals and plants that died a very long time ago and became preserved in rocks. These remains are our 'window on the past'. They show us the amazing variety of life that thrived and then disappeared over millions of years of Earth's history.

▲ A preserved rhinoceros skeleton gradually emerges from ten-million-year-old rocks at a fossil excavation or 'dig' in Nebraska, USA. Removing the remains is just the first part of recreating how this great beast looked, lived and died.

What are fossils?

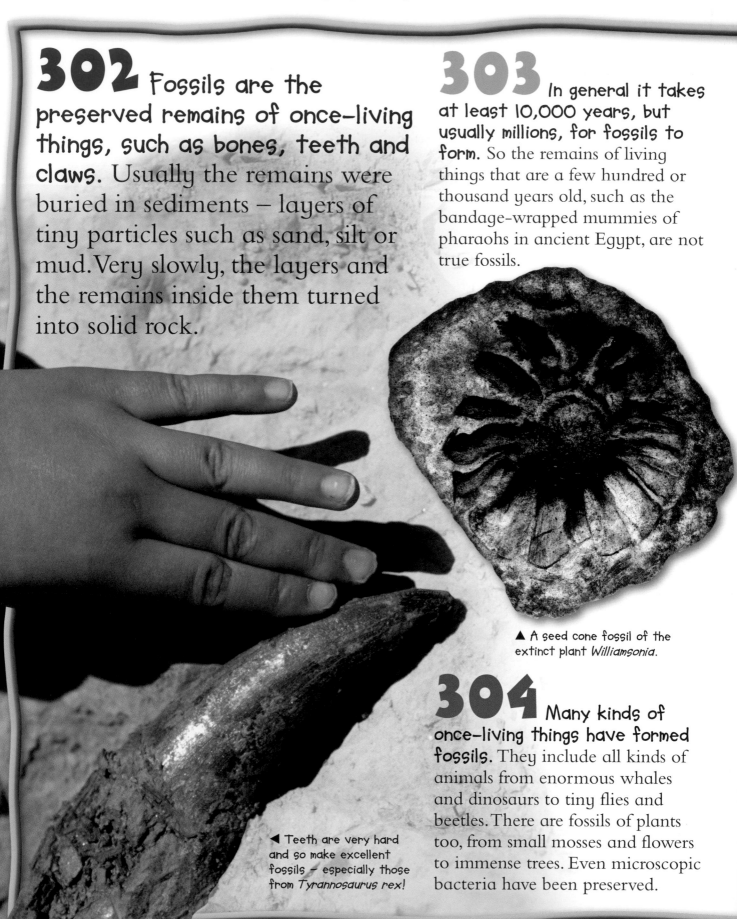

302 Fossils are the preserved remains of once-living things, such as bones, teeth and claws. Usually the remains were buried in sediments – layers of tiny particles such as sand, silt or mud. Very slowly, the layers and the remains inside them turned into solid rock.

303 In general it takes at least 10,000 years, but usually millions, for fossils to form. So the remains of living things that are a few hundred or thousand years old, such as the bandage-wrapped mummies of pharaohs in ancient Egypt, are not true fossils.

▲ A seed cone fossil of the extinct plant *Williamsonia*.

304 Many kinds of once-living things have formed fossils. They include all kinds of animals from enormous whales and dinosaurs to tiny flies and beetles. There are fossils of plants too, from small mosses and flowers to immense trees. Even microscopic bacteria have been preserved.

◄ Teeth are very hard and so make excellent fossils – especially those from *Tyrannosaurus rex*!

▶ It is unusual for thin, delicate bones, such as those of the bat *Icaronycteris*, to fossilize.

305 In most cases, fossils formed from the hard parts of living things that did not rot away soon after death. As well as bones, teeth and claws these include shells, scales and the bark, roots, cones and seeds of plants.

306 Much more rarely, soft parts have been preserved as fossils, such as flower petals and worm bodies. Where this has happened, it gives a fascinating glimpse into how these ancient life-forms looked and lived.

▼ The tube worms' soft bodies soon decayed but their hard, coiled tubes were preserved in the seabed mud.

QUIZ

Which of these are true fossils?
A. A bird called the dodo, which died out over 300 years ago
B. Two-thousand-year-old pots and vases from ancient Rome
C. The first shellfish that appeared in the sea over 500 million years ago

Answer:
C is a true fossil.
The others are much too recent.

137

Fossils in myth and legend

307 Centuries ago, the word 'fossil' was used for anything dug out of the ground. This included strange-shaped rocks, crystals and gold nuggets. However 'fossil' gradually came to mean the remains of once-living plants or animals.

▲ Fossilized *Gryphea* oyster shells were known as 'devil's toenails' due to their curved shape.

308 Long ago, some people regarded fossils as rocks and stones that had been specially shaped by gods to resemble animal teeth, tree bark and similar items. People believed this could be to show the gods' great powers and to test the faith of believers.

▶ It was once believed that ammonites (prehistoric sea creatures) were snakes that had turned to stone. This ammonite fossil has had a snake's head carved on it.

I DON'T BELIEVE IT!

The ancient Greeks likened ammonite fossils to coiled goat horns, believing them to be sacred because they associated them with the horned god, Jupiter Ammon.

309 In some parts of the world, fossils were seen as the remains of animals that perished in a terrible catastrophe. An example was the Great Flood as described in the Bible. A man named Noah managed to save many creatures by building an ark, but most perished in the rising waters.

◄ Bird or dinosaur? This small dinosaur was preserved with its body covering of feathers.

310 In ancient China, people once regarded fossils as the remains of dragons, giant serpents and similar monsters. Modern science shows that such animals never existed, but they seemed very real to people many years ago because they featured in tales of myth and legend.

311 Some fossils had their own myths. Rod-like fossils with pointed ends come from inside the bodies of belemnites, which were prehistoric relatives of squid. They were called 'thunderstones' from the belief that they formed when lightning hit the ground.

► Belemnites were ancient sea creatures related to cuttlefish and octopuses. The fossilized pointed shell from inside the body is sometimes called a 'belemnite bullet'.

Fossils get scientific

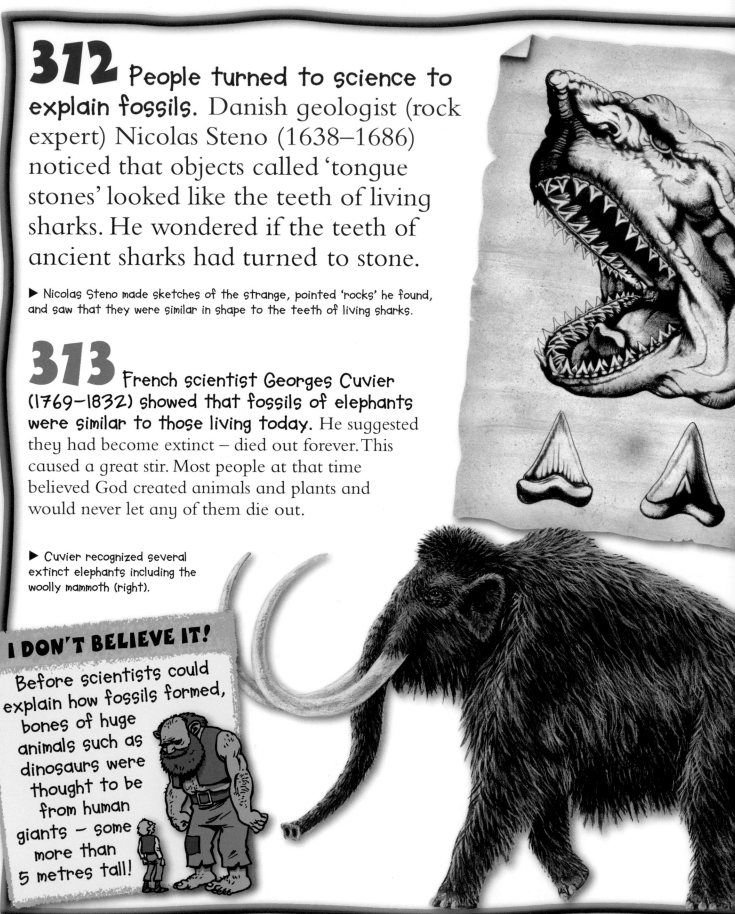

312 **People turned to science to explain fossils.** Danish geologist (rock expert) Nicolas Steno (1638–1686) noticed that objects called 'tongue stones' looked like the teeth of living sharks. He wondered if the teeth of ancient sharks had turned to stone.

▶ Nicolas Steno made sketches of the strange, pointed 'rocks' he found, and saw that they were similar in shape to the teeth of living sharks.

313 **French scientist Georges Cuvier (1769–1832) showed that fossils of elephants were similar to those living today.** He suggested they had become extinct – died out forever. This caused a great stir. Most people at that time believed God created animals and plants and would never let any of them die out.

▶ Cuvier recognized several extinct elephants including the woolly mammoth (right).

I DON'T BELIEVE IT!

Before scientists could explain how fossils formed, bones of huge animals such as dinosaurs were thought to be from human giants – some more than 5 metres tall!

314 In the 1820s, English doctor Gideon Mantell (1790–1852) found some huge fossil teeth similar to those of the iguana lizard, but **bigger.** He called the beast they came from *Iguanodon.* This was the first dinosaur to be named. Soon the search was on for fossils of more dinosaurs and other extinct animals.

315 In 1859, English naturalist Charles Darwin (1809–1882) published his book *On The Origin of Species.* In it, Darwin suggested that species (kinds) of living things that could not succeed in the struggle for survival died out or changed into new kinds, leaving fossils on the way.

316 In the 1800s, palaeontology became a new and important branch of science. This is the study of prehistoric life and it relies greatly on fossils of all kinds.

◀ Darwin examined fossils of the giant sloth *Megatherium* and wrote: "Existing animals have a close relation in form to extinct species."

How fossils form

▼ All living things die. Those living in water, such as this ichthyosaur, are more likely to leave fossils than those on land.

317 When a living thing dies, its flesh and other soft parts start to rot. Sometimes they are eaten by scavenging creatures such as worms and insects. The harder parts, such as teeth and bones, rot more slowly and last longer.

318 Fossil formation usually begins like this, and very often in water. Sediments tend to settle on dead animals and plants in ponds, lakes, rivers and seas. This is the main reason why most fossils are of plants and animals that lived in water or somehow got washed into water.

1. After death, the ichthyosaur sinks to the seabed. Worms, crabs and other scavengers eat its soft body parts.

START SOME FOSSILS

You will need:
small stones   glass mixing jug
sand   water

Imagine the stones are 'bones' of an ancient creature. They get washed into a river – put them in the jug and half-fill with water. Then the 'bones' are covered by sediment – sprinkle in the sand.

320 Water trickles into the sediments and once–living remains. The water contains dissolved substances such as minerals and salts. Gradually, these replace the once-living parts and turn them and the sediments into solid rock. This is called permineralization.

321 Most living things rot away soon after death, so the chances of anything becoming a fossil are slim. Also, sedimentary rock layers change over time, becoming heated and bent, which can destroy fossils in them. The chances of anyone finding a fossil are even tinier. This is why the record of fossils in rocks represents only a tiny proportion of prehistoric life.

319 Over time, more sediment layers settle on top of the remains. As they are covered deeper, further rotting or scavenging is less likely.

2. Sediments cover the hard body parts, such as bones and teeth, which gradually turn into solid rock.

3. Millions of years later the upper rock layers wear away and the fossil remains are exposed.

Mould and cast fossils

322 Because of the way fossils form, they are almost always found in sedimentary rocks such as sandstone, limestone, chalk, shale and slate. Other kinds of rocks, such as igneous rocks that cool from red-hot, runny lava erupted from volcanoes, do not contain fossils.

▼ Ammonites were fierce hunting animals related to squid. They died out with the dinosaurs 65 million years ago.

Cast fossil

Mould fossil

▲ This ammonite fossil has split into part and counterpart, with a mould and cast fossil inside.

323 As the bits and pieces of sediments become solid rock, the once-living remains within them may not. They are dissolved by water and gradually washed away. The result is a hole in the rock the same shape as the remains, called a mould fossil.

324 After more time, the hole or mould in the rock may fill with minerals deposited by water. This produces a lump of stone that is different in make-up from the surrounding rocks, but is the same shape as the original remains. This is known as a cast fossil.

325

Moulds and casts form with a whole fossil, and also with holes and spaces within a fossil. For example, the fossil skull of an animal may have a space inside where the brain once was. If this fills with minerals it can form a lump of rock that is the same size and shape as the original brain. These types of cast fossils are known as endocasts.

326

Usually, the slower fossilization happens, the more details it preserves of the original living parts. Incredible tiny features are shown even under the microscope.

▲ Sometimes many animals are fossilized together. Perhaps these fish were trapped when the water they were in dried up. Their remains show amazing detail.

I DON'T BELIEVE IT!

Fossil skulls of the ancient humans called Neanderthals show that many of them had bigger brains than people of today!

Special preservation

▲ This frog dried out before its flesh could rot away, leaving its mummified remains.

327 Once-living things can be preserved in many different ways. Mummification is when a dead plant or animal is left to dry out slowly. Some dinosaurs and animals have been preserved in this way in the windblown sands of deserts.

328 Amber is the sap (sticky resin) from prehistoric trees, especially conifers, that has been fossilized. If small creatures became trapped by the resin, they are preserved within it. Insects, spiders, frogs, and even leaves and seeds have all been preserved in this way.

◀ Amber preserves amazingly small details, even the delicate wings of this fly.

329 Natural pools of thick, sticky tar ooze up from the ground in some places such as forests and scrubland. Animals that become trapped sink into the tar pit and may be preserved – even huge creatures such as wolves, deer, bears, sabre-tooth cats and mammoths.

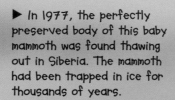

▶ In 1977, the perfectly preserved body of this baby mammoth was found thawing out in Siberia. The mammoth had been trapped in ice for thousands of years.

330 Being naturally frozen into the ice of the far north or south is a type of preservation. It's not true fossilization, but as the ice melts it reveals deep-frozen flowers, trees, mammoths and deer.

◀ Fossilized human footprints in southeastern Australia. The spacing of fossil footprints, called trackways, show how their makers walked and ran.

MATCH-UP!

Match the following with how they were preserved.
A. Desert-living dinosaur
B. Wolf in woodland
C. Tree-dwelling insect

1. Natural tar pit
2. Trapped in amber
3. Mummification.

Answers:
A3 B1 C2

331 Trace fossils are not actual body parts of once-living things. They are signs or 'traces' made by them, which then became fossilized. Examples include the footprints of animals, their burrows, egg shells, teeth marks and scratch marks, which can all turn to stone.

Fossils from jelly

332 Some rare and exciting fossils were not formed from the hard parts of living things. They were once soft creatures such as worms, jellyfish and anemones, preserved in unusual conditions.

333 Almost all living things need oxygen to survive. In some kinds of seabed mud, the water is still and brings no oxygen, so there is no life. If sea animals and plants end up here, maybe after an underwater mudslide, there are no living things to rot them in the usual way.

334 In oxygen-less conditions, dead, soft-bodied creatures and plants gradually undergo a strange type of fossilization into carbon films and impressions. These are like smears of oil or powder in the rock. They occur especially in sedimentary rocks called shales or mudstones.

◄ Jellyfish are soft and floppy, but they have on rare occasions left fossilized impressions in sand and mud.

◄ This fossil, called *Mawsonites*, may have been a jellyfish, the root-like holdfast of a seaweed or an animal's burrow network in the mud.

335
About 505 million years ago some seabed mud slid and slumped into deep, oxygen-free water. The black shale rocks that formed are at Burgess Pass in the Rocky Mountains of British Columbia, Canada.

QUIZ

1. Name a gas that most living things need to survive.
2. What type of rock is mudstone?
3. Of all the types of animals and plants that have ever lived, how many have died out?

Answers:
1. Oxygen 2. Sedimentary 3. 999 out of 1000

336
Burgess Shale fossils number **many tens of thousands.** They include the strangest kinds of creatures resembling worms, jellyfish and shrimps. Some are like no other animals ever known.

▼ The Burgess Shale area is a World Heritage Site. It has yielded more than 60,000 fossils from the Cambrian Period, 582–488 million years ago.

337
Rare fossils give a tiny glimpse into the myriad of creatures that thrived long ago, but are rarely preserved. They show that of all the kinds of animals and plants that have ever lived, more than 999 out of 1000 are extinct (died out).

Fossils and time

338 Fossils are studied by many kinds of scientists. Palaeontologists are general experts on fossils and prehistoric life. Palaeozoologists specialize in prehistoric creatures, and palaeobotanists in prehistoric plants. Geologists study rocks, soil and other substances that make up the Earth. All of these sciences allow us to work out the immense prehistory of the Earth.

339 Earth's existence is divided into enormous lengths of time called eons, which are split into eras, then periods, epochs and finally, stages. Each of these time divisions is marked by changes in the rocks formed at the time – and if the rocks are sedimentary, by the fossils they contain. The whole time span, from the formation of the Earth 4600 million years ago to today, is known as the geological time scale.

▼ Starting with the Cambrian Period (far right), this timeline shows 11 major time periods in Earth's history. It gives examples of some of the fossil animals and plants that have been found for each period. 'MYA' stands for 'millions of years ago'.

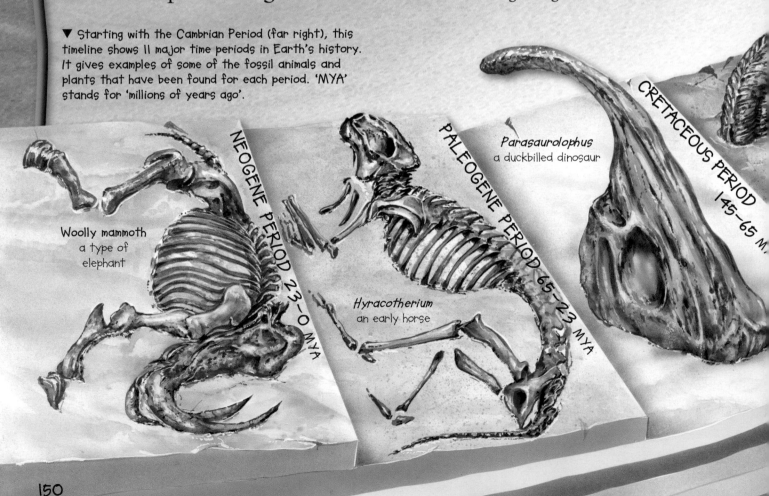

Woolly mammoth
a type of elephant

NEOGENE PERIOD 23–0 MYA

Hyracotherium
an early horse

PALEOGENE PERIOD 65–23 MYA

Parasaurolophus
a duckbilled dinosaur

CRETACEOUS PERIOD 145–65 M...

CAMBRIAN PERIOD 542–488 MYA

Trilobite
a shelled marine creature

ORDOVICIAN PERIOD 488–444 MYA

SILURIAN PERIOD 444–416 MYA

DEVONIAN PERIOD 416–359 MYA

340 An example of a geological time division is the Cretaceous Period, from 145 to 65 million years ago. It is named after creta or *kreta*, a Latin word for chalk. Due to temperature, rainfall and other climate conditions, layers of chalk rocks formed. They contained fossils such as certain kinds of shellfish, the winged reptiles known as pterosaurs and many kinds of dinosaurs.

Graptolite
a simple marine animal

Birkenia
a type of fish

Crinoid
a simple marine animal

CARBONIFEROUS PERIOD 359–299 MYA

PERMIAN PERIOD 299–251 MYA

Lepidodendron
a primitive tree

TRIASSIC PERIOD 251–200 MYA

Diplocaulus
an early amphibian

JURASSIC PERIOD 200–145 MYA

Rhamphorhynchus
a winged reptile

Stephanoceras
a type of ammonite

MAKE CHALK FOSSILS

You will need:
chalk sticks   metal teaspoon

Chalk often contains fossil shellfish. Find pictures of long, thin examples, such as razorshells, mussels and belemnites. Use the spoon to scrape and carve the chalk sticks into shapes to make your own 'fossil' museum.

Working out dates

341 'Dating' a fossil means finding out how old it is. Usually, rocks found deeper in the ground are older than the rock layers above them, so any fossils they contain are also older. Sedimentary rock layers and their fossils have been compared to build up a picture of which fossilized plants and animals lived when.

342 If a new fossil is found, it can be compared with this overall pattern to get an idea of its age. This is known as relative dating – finding the date of a fossil relative to other fossils of known ages.

▼ Different rock layers can be clearly seen in the Grand Canyon, USA. The layers have been revealed by the Colorado River as it winds its way through the canyon.

▲ Some types of chalk rocks are almost entirely made of the fossils of small sea creatures.

343 Certain types of plants and animals were very common, survived for millions of years and left plenty of fossil remains. This makes them extremely useful for relative dating. They are known as marker, index, indicator, guide or zone fossils.

344 Most index fossils come from the sea, where preservation is more likely than on land. They include multi-legged trilobites, curly-shelled ammonites, ball-shaped echinoids (sea urchins) and net-like graptolites. On land, tough pollen grains and spores from plants are useful index fossils.

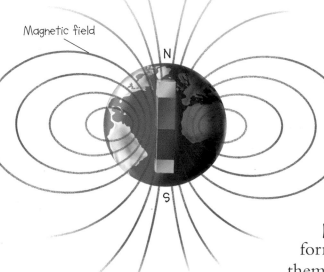

Magnetic field

N

S

▲ Earth's magnetism has changed and even reversed over millions of years, helping to date fossils.

▶ Trilobites make good index fossils. Different kinds appeared and then died out between 530 million and about 250 million years ago.

345 Earth's natural magnetic field changed many times through prehistory. When some kinds of igneous rocks formed by cooling, the magnetism was 'frozen' into them, known as palaeomagnetism. It can be dated by comparison with the whole pattern of magnetic changes through Earth's history.

How many years ago?

346 Relative dating, by comparing fossils with each other, shows if one fossil is older or younger than another. But how do we know the actual age of fossils in millions of years, known as absolute dating?

347 The main kind of absolute dating is based on naturally occurring substances that give off tiny amounts of rays and particles, known as radioactivity. As they give off these weak forms of energy, the substances – known as radioisotopes – change or 'decay' slightly. The amounts of different radioisotopes in a fossil can be measured to show how long ago it formed. This is known as radiometric dating.

348 Several kinds of substances are used for radiometric dating. Each decays at a set rate, some slower than others. Very slow ones are useful for the oldest fossils, and the fastest ones for young fossils.

◄ The rocks of the Canadian Shield, a huge area of land in eastern and central Canada, have been dated to more than 2500 million years ago.

349 Radiocarbon dating is based on the change or decay of one form of carbon known as C14. It happens relatively fast and is useful for a time span up to 60,000 years ago. This helps with dating young fossils and with items such as deep-frozen mammoths.

350 In potassium–argon dating, the element potassium changes into argon very slowly, over billions of years. It's useful for rock layers formed just above or below fossils from billions of years ago to about 100,000 years ago. Rubidium-strontium and uranium-lead dating can reveal the age of even older rocks, almost back to when Earth began.

▼ Geologists measure tiny amounts of radioactivity in rocks and fossils using equipment such as Geiger counters.

▼ Radiocarbon dating.

1. Woolly mammoth eats plants containing C14

2. Mammoth dies, no more C14 is taken in

3. Half of C14 decays every 5730 years

Fossil-hunting takes off

351 **From the early 19th century, fossil-hunting became more popular.** Towns and cities as well as rich individuals began to establish museums and collections of the 'wonders of nature' with displays of stuffed animals, pinned insects, pressed flowers – and lots of fossils.

352 **People began to earn a living by finding and selling fossils.** One of the first was Mary Anning (1799–1847) of Lyme Regis, southern England. For many years she collected fossils from the seashore, where waves and storms regularly cracked open boulders and cliffs to reveal new finds. Mary discovered fossil fish, ichthyosaurs, plesiosaurs, pterosaurs and many other animals.

▶ As in Mary Anning's time, fossils still appear from the rocks at Lyme Regis.

353 In 1881, the British Museum opened its display of natural history collections in London, which showed fossils and similar wonders from around the world. Other great cities had similar museums and sent fossil-hunters to remote places for the most spectacular finds.

▲ By the 1860s many museums had fossils on display, such as this 'sea serpent' or mosasaur.

▼ Cope and Marsh found and described about 130 new kinds of dinosaurs.

Othniel Charles Marsh

Edward Drinker Cope

354 Between the 1870s and 1890s, two of the leading fossil-hunters were Americans Othniel Charles Marsh and Edward Drinker Cope. Their teams tried to outdo each other to discover the most and best fossil dinosaurs, as well as other animals and plants too.

▲ The first fossil stegosaur skulls were found in the 1870s.

▶ The dinosaur *Stegosaurus* was named by Marsh in 1877.

355 From the early 1900s fossil-hunting spread to Africa and then in the 1920s to Mongolia and China. From the 1970s there were finds in South America and Australia. Today, fossil-hunters go all over the world in search of new discoveries.

Famous hot spots

356 Some places around the world have become famous for their fossils. These places are often in the news because of dinosaur remains. However dinosaur finds are only some of the thousands of fossils being unearthed and studied.

▼ This map shows some of the most famous fossil sites around the world.

357 The Midwest 'Badlands' of North America has many famous fossil sites. At Dinosaur National Monument, on the border between Colorado and Utah, USA, the rocks date to almost 150 million years ago. Apart from dinosaur remains they also yield fossils of crocodiles, turtles, frogs, shellfish and plants.

USA
Dinosaur National Monument

◀ Dinosaur fossils at Dinosaur National Monument. This park opened in 1915 and receives over 350,000 visitors each year.

BRAZIL
Santana Formation

358 In northeast Brazil in South America there are limestone rocks about 110–90 million years old known as the Santana Formation. Detailed fossils include pterosaurs, reptiles, frogs, insects and plants. Some fossil fish were preserved with the remains of their last meals inside their bodies.

◀ This 100-million-year-old dragonfly is one of thousands from Brazil's Santana Formation rocks.

359 Some of the best European fossils come from limestone quarries around Solnhofen, southern Germany. There are dinosaurs, pterosaurs, the earliest known bird *Archaeopteryx*, fish, insects and soft-bodied jellyfish.

▲ One of the smallest dinosaurs, *Compsognathus* has been preserved in amazing detail at Solnhofen, Germany.

GERMANY
● Solnhofen

EGYPT

Fayoum

360 Lightning Ridge is in northwest New South Wales, Australia. As well as beautiful black opal gemstones there are fossils 110 million years old of long-gone mammals, dinosaurs, pterosaurs, crocodiles, turtles, sharks, crayfish, snails, shellfish and pine cones.

AUSTRALIA

Lightning Ridge

▲ Fossils of more than 400 whales such as *Basilosaurus* are known from Egypt's Fayoum area.

361 Fayoum, south of Cairo in Egypt, is one of Africa's best fossil sites. There are remains 40–25 million years old of prehistoric mammals such as hippos, rhinos, elephants, rats, bats, monkeys and even whales.

▲ Fossils of the giant wombat *Diprotodon* have been found in Australia.

Looking for fossils

362 **Where do we find fossils?** Fossil-hunters use many kinds of aids and clues to find the best sites. Geological maps show which kinds of rocks are found at or just under the surface. To contain fossils, these rocks need to be sedimentary, such as limestone.

363 **Fossil-hunters are careful to get permission to search a site.** The landowner, land manager and local authorities must all agree on the search methods and the ownership of any finds. This avoids problems such as trespassing, criminal damage and 'fossil-rustling' (stealing).

▶ Palaeontologists sift through rocks and common fossils for signs of important specimens at Bromacker Quarry, Germany.

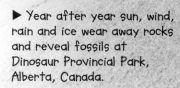
▶ Year after year sun, wind, rain and ice wear away rocks and reveal fossils at Dinosaur Provincial Park, Alberta, Canada.

364 Good places to look for fossils are where rocks are regularly broken apart and worn away by waves, wind, sun, ice and other weather. This is the process of erosion. It happens at cliffs, seashores, river banks and valleys, canyons and caves. It also happens where people dig quarries, mines, road and railway cuttings and building foundations.

365 Satellite images, aerial photographs, survey trips by plane, or even just walking around show the nature of the ground. Bare rocky areas are best, rather than areas covered with soil, plants and trees.

▶ This satellite photo of East Africa's Olduvai Gorge shows one of the world's best areas for prehistoric human fossils.

366 Fossil-hunters also follow a collector's code of guidelines. These show how to cause the least damage when digging, how to stay safe and how to restore the site afterwards. Find out more about this by logging on to the following web address: http://www.discovering fossils.co.uk/fossil_hunting_guidelines.htm

At the dig

367 Some people look for fossils in their spare time and if they find one it's a bonus. At an important site, scientists such as palaeontologists organize an excavation or 'dig' that can last for many months.

368 The dig area is divided into squares called a grid, usually by string or strips of wood. This is used to record the positions of the finds. As the excavation continues, the workers make notes, take photographs, draw sketches and use many other recording methods.

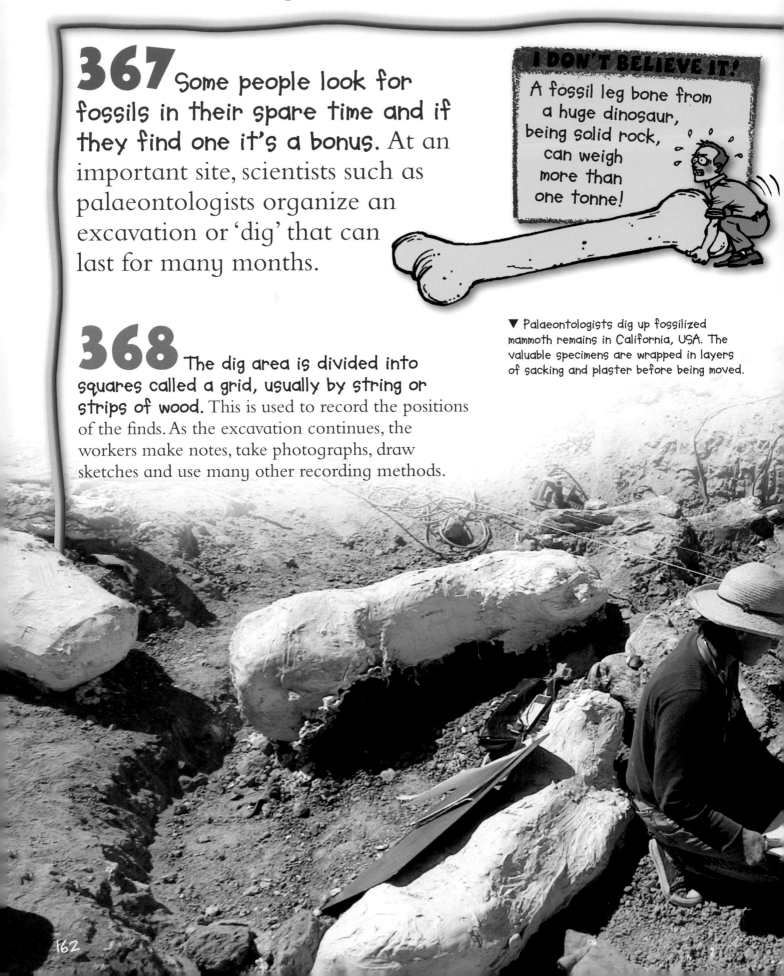

▼ Palaeontologists dig up fossilized mammoth remains in California, USA. The valuable specimens are wrapped in layers of sacking and plaster before being moved.

369 At first there may be lots of loose rocks, boulders or soil to remove, called overburden. Big, powerful tools might be used such as mechanical diggers, road drills (jackhammers) or even dynamite!

▲ It can take weeks to clean a large fossil such as this elephant skull and tusk.

370 As fossils are exposed, experts decide whether they are worth digging out. Gradually the excavation methods become more careful, using hammers, chisels, small picks and brushes to avoid damaging the find. It can be a lengthy, difficult task. The dig site might be a baking desert, tropical swamp or freezing mountainside.

371 Small bits of loose rock might be sieved to find tiny fossils. Soft, fragile fossils can be covered with material such as plaster or fibre-glass, which hardens into a protective jacket. This allows the fossil to be lifted out.

163

Cleaning up fossils

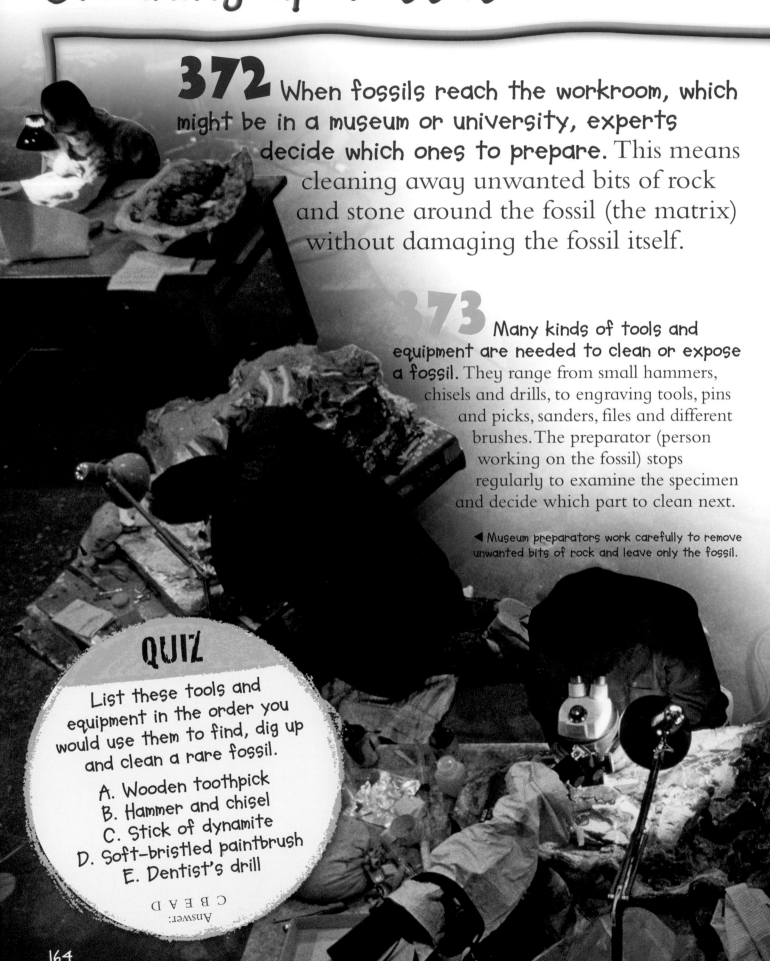

372 When fossils reach the workroom, which might be in a museum or university, experts decide which ones to prepare. This means cleaning away unwanted bits of rock and stone around the fossil (the matrix) without damaging the fossil itself.

373 Many kinds of tools and equipment are needed to clean or expose a fossil. They range from small hammers, chisels and drills, to engraving tools, pins and picks, sanders, files and different brushes. The preparator (person working on the fossil) stops regularly to examine the specimen and decide which part to clean next.

◄ Museum preparators work carefully to remove unwanted bits of rock and leave only the fossil.

QUIZ

List these tools and equipment in the order you would use them to find, dig up and clean a rare fossil.

A. Wooden toothpick
B. Hammer and chisel
C. Stick of dynamite
D. Soft-bristled paintbrush
E. Dentist's drill

Answer:
C B E A D

374 Microscopes are often used to show tiny details of a fossil during preparation. Usually this is a stereoscopic microscope with two eyepieces, like binoculars, mounted on a stand with the specimen beneath.

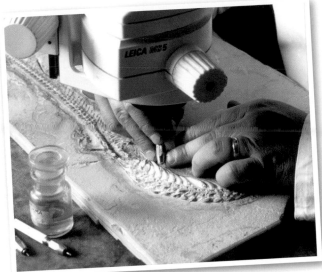

▲ The enlarged view through a stereo microscope shows lots of detail, to avoid scratching or chipping the specimen.

▶ It may take a year to dissolve rock with acid and expose the fossils – these are unhatched dinosaur eggs.

Dinosaur embryo

375 When the fossil is one type of rock and the matrix is another, preparators may use chemicals to expose the fossil. Different acids are tested on small parts of the matrix and fossil, to see if they dissolve the former but not the latter.

376 Very few animals or plants die neatly in one piece and are preserved whole. So it's incredibly rare to find a whole fossilized plant or animal with all the parts positioned as they were in life. Most fossils are bits and pieces that are crushed and distorted. Putting them back together is very difficult!

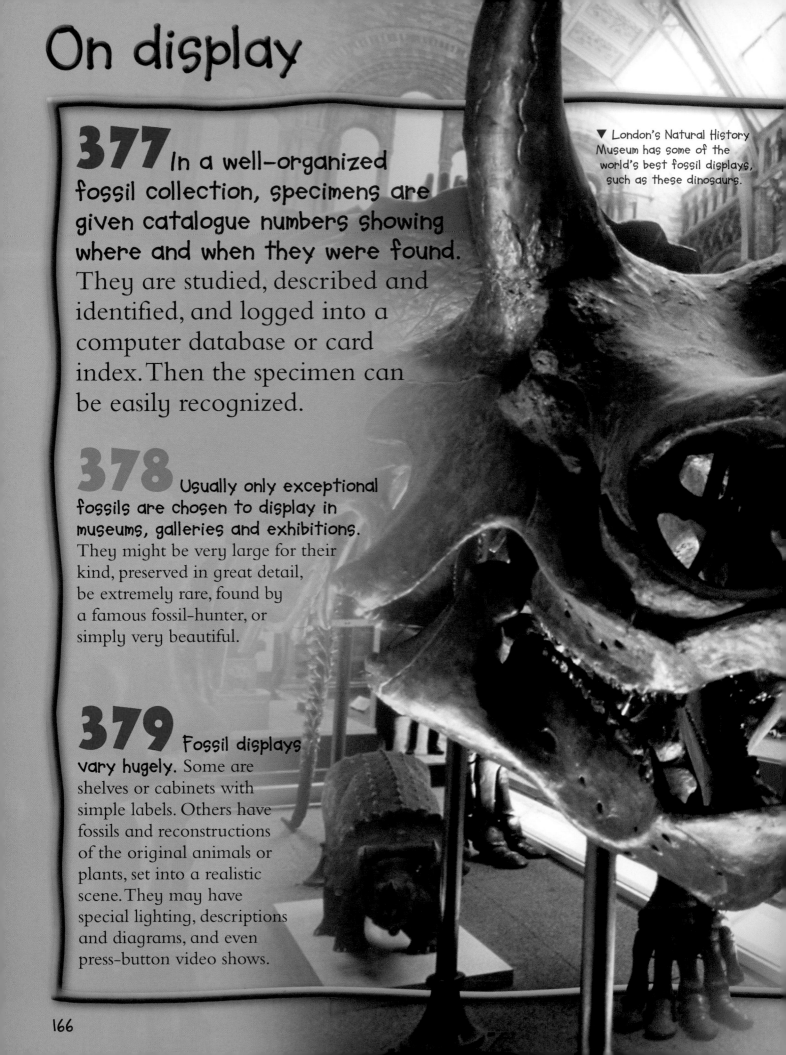

On display

377 In a well-organized fossil collection, specimens are given catalogue numbers showing where and when they were found. They are studied, described and identified, and logged into a computer database or card index. Then the specimen can be easily recognized.

378 Usually only exceptional fossils are chosen to display in museums, galleries and exhibitions. They might be very large for their kind, preserved in great detail, be extremely rare, found by a famous fossil-hunter, or simply very beautiful.

379 Fossil displays vary hugely. Some are shelves or cabinets with simple labels. Others have fossils and reconstructions of the original animals or plants, set into a realistic scene. They may have special lighting, descriptions and diagrams, and even press-button video shows.

▼ London's Natural History Museum has some of the world's best fossil displays, such as these dinosaurs.

380 Some fossils are so rare, delicate or valuable that they are not displayed – copies are. Copies or replicas of very rare fossils might be sent to other museums so more people can study them.

381 Copies are used for big creatures such as dinosaurs, whales and mammoths. The original fossils are solid rock and can weigh many tonnes. Lightweight copies are easier and safer to put on a frame or hang by wires, to build up the animal in a lifelike position.

Fossils come alive!

382 One of the most exciting parts of fossil study is to reconstruct (rebuild) the original plant or animal. This needs a detailed knowledge of anatomy, or body structure. For example, fossils of prehistoric birds are compared to the same body parts of similar birds alive today. This is called comparative anatomy.

383 Tiny marks or 'scars' on fossil bones show where the animal's muscles attached in real life. These help to reveal muscle shapes and arrangements so experts can gradually put the flesh on the (fossil) bones.

Fossil bones
Faint scars on fossil bones can help scientists work out how and where muscles were attached

▲ This reconstruction of an ankylosaur, an armoured dinosaur, is being done head-first. The tail is still bare fossils of the bones.

384 We can see how a living creature walks, runs and jumps using the joints between its bones. If fossil bones have their joints preserved, their detailed shapes and designs show the range of motion and how the animal moved.

MULTI-COLOURED BIRD

You will need:
pictures of *Archaeopteryx*   colour pens
tracing paper   white paper

No one knows what colour the first bird *Archaeopteryx* was. Look at pictures of it in books and on web sites. See how its feather colours and patterns differ. Trace an outline of *Archaeopteryx* from a book and colour it to your own amazing design.

Soft tissues
Flesh, guts and muscles can be added
to the skeleton as scientists compare
the fossil to similar living animals

Skin
The external covering of skin,
scales, horns and claws are added
by studying fossil examples and
using intelligent guess work

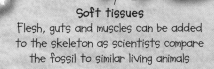

386 The outward appearance
of an animal might be known from fossils
such as an outer shell, scaly skin,
feathers or fur. However fossils are not
original living parts – they have changed to
rock. So the colour of fossil skin is the
colour of the type of rock, not the animal.
Experts guess at colours and patterns for
their reconstructions.

385 Gradually, soft parts
such as the guts of an animal or the
petals of a flower, can be guessed
and added to the reconstruction.
Again, experts use information from
fossil relatives and living cousins.

Trading, stealing, faking

387 Fossils are big business. Thousands of people work at digs, in workrooms and in museums, exhibitions and galleries. A find such as a new dinosaur can hit the news headlines and make the discoverer famous – and rich!

388 The biggest, most complete fossil *Tyrannosaurus rex* was found in 1990 near Faith, Dakota, by Sue Hendrickson. The dinosaur was nicknamed 'Sue' and there was a long legal dispute about who owned it. Finally it was sold to the Field Museum of Chicago for more than seven million dollars!

◀ Street traders offer fossils for sale in North Africa. There is no guarantee the fossils came from the local area.

▶ Chinese palaeontologist Dong Zhiming with some smuggled dinosaur eggs. Every year police, customs and security staff uncover illegal collections such as this.

389 Real fossils, replicas and models are sold around the world by museums, shops, mail-order catalogues and on the Internet. Buyers range from leading museums to individuals who like the idea of a home fossil collection without the trouble of digging them up.

▼ Rare or unusual fossils, such as this ammonite shell showing detailed internal structure, can fetch huge sums of money at auction.

390 Stealing and faking fossils has been going on for centuries. In 1999 scientists announced a fossil creature called *Archaeoraptor* that seemed to be part-bird and part-dinosaur. *Archaeoraptor* showed how small meat-eating dinosaurs evolved into birds. However further study revealed that the specimen was indeed part-dinosaur and part-bird, because it was a fake with separate fossils cleverly glued together.

Famous fossils

391 Many fossils and prehistoric sites around the world are massive attractions, visited by millions of people. The Petrified Forest National Park in Arizona, USA has hundreds of huge fossilized trees and smaller specimens of animals such as dinosaurs, dating from about 225 million years ago. It receives more than half a million visitors yearly.

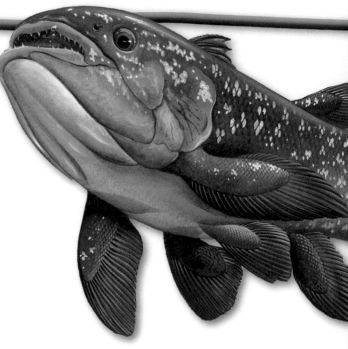

▲ The coelacanth is known as a 'living fossil', meaning it is very similar to its long-extinct relatives.

392 The coelacanth fish was known only from fossils and thought to have been extinct for more than 60 million years. In 1938 a living coelacanth was caught off southeast Africa and more have been discovered since. Living things that are very similar to their prehistoric relatives are known as 'living fossils'.

▶ Thousands of fossil tree trunks and branches litter the ground at Arizona's Petrified Forest National Park.

393
There are only about ten fossils of *Archaeopteryx*, the first known bird. All come from the Solnhofen area of southern Germany. They are amazingly detailed and almost priceless.

▶ Each specimen of *Archaeopteryx* is closely guarded.

394
'Lucy' is a fossilized part-skeleton from a very early human-type creature. It was discovered in 1974 in Ethiopia, Africa and dates back about 3.2 million years. Thousands of people flock to see 'her' every year.

◀ Piltdown Man was really the skull of a human from about 500 years ago combined with the jawbone of an orang-utan.

I DON'T BELIEVE IT!
Animal droppings can become fossils known as coprolites. Leftovers in them can show what an animal ate. Luckily they are no longer squishy and smelly, but have become solid rock.

395
Piltdown Man is perhaps the most famous fossil fake. It was found in southeast England in 1912 and thought to be an early kind of human. In 1953 it was exposed as a hoax by new scientific methods.

Looking to the future

396 As fossil–hunting goes on around the world, scientific methods and equipment grow more powerful. Ground-penetrating radar, X-rays and CT (computerized tomography) scanners can 'see' fossils inside solid rock.

▲ A CT scanner examines the fossil skull of an ancient type of otter.

397 As we improve ways to study fossils, old specimens are looked at again to see new details. The dinosaur *Oviraptor* or 'egg thief' was named because one of its fossils suggested it was stealing the eggs of another dinosaur. Then X-rays of similar eggs showed baby *Oviraptor*s inside. The 'egg thief' fossil was probably looking after its own eggs.

◄ This *Oviraptor* may have died shielding its eggs from a predator, 75 million years ago.

398 Some amazing fossils of the 1990s–2000s are from Liaoning Province in northeast China. They date to 130 million years ago, and show details of creatures and plants, including dinosaurs with feathers and a cat-sized mammal that preyed on baby dinosaurs.

▲ Fossils of the tiny feathered dinosaur *Microraptor* have been found in China.

399 New fossils provide more evidence for evolution, such as how fish changed gradually into land animals. *Panderichthys* was a fish-like creature from 380 million years ago. It had features such as finger-like bones developing in its fins.

400 Important fossil discoveries cause news and excitement around the world. They affect our ideas about prehistoric life, how Earth has changed through time, evolution and extinction. They can also help to fill in the details of where we came from.

QUIZ

Match these nicknames of fossils with their scientific names.
A. 'Lucy' B. 'Stan' C. 'Jaws'
D. 'Spike'
1. Triceratops (dinosaur)
2. Megalodon (giant shark)
3. Australopithecus afarensis (early human)
4. Tyrannosaurus (dinosaur)

Answers:
A3 B4 C2 D1

▲ *Panderichthys* was about one metre long. Its fossils come from Latvia in northeastern Europe.

EXTINCT

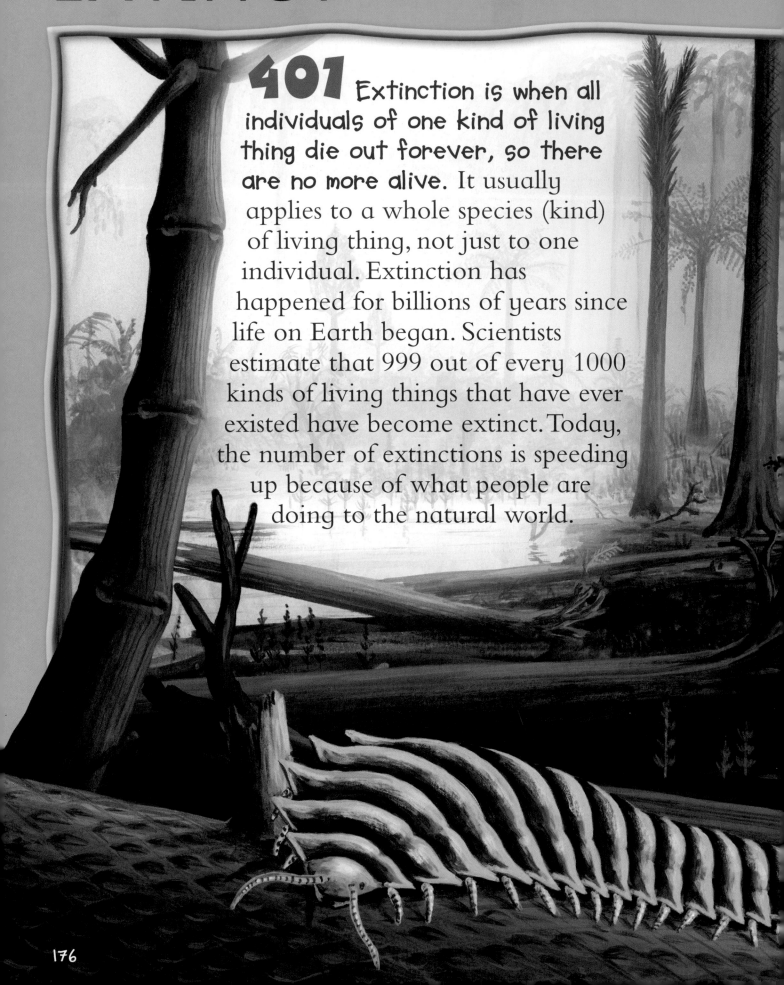

401 Extinction is when all individuals of one kind of living thing die out forever, so there are no more alive. It usually applies to a whole species (kind) of living thing, not just to one individual. Extinction has happened for billions of years since life on Earth began. Scientists estimate that 999 out of every 1000 kinds of living things that have ever existed have become extinct. Today, the number of extinctions is speeding up because of what people are doing to the natural world.

▼ Giant dragonflies, millipedes as big as dining tables and enormous tree ferns once inhabited forests 300 million years ago. However all of the creatures in this prehistoric swamp have long been extinct.

What is extinction?

402 Extinction is the dying out of a particular kind, or type, of living thing. It is gone forever and can never come back (although this may change in the future). Extinction affects plants such as flowers and trees, as well as fungi such as mushrooms and moulds. It also affects tiny worms and bugs, and big creatures such as dinosaurs and mammoths.

▲ The 'terror bird' *Phorusrhacos* lived ten million years ago. Nothing like it survives today.

403 Extinction is linked to how we classify (group) living things. It usually applies to a species. A species includes all living things that look similar and breed to produce more of their kind. For instance, all lions belong to one species, which scientists call *Panthera leo*.

QUIZ

Which of these could, perhaps, one day become extinct?
1. Great white sharks 2. Robots
3. Daisies 4. Cameras with rolls of film (not digital)
5. Satellites 6. Houseflies

Answers:
Only living things can become extinct, so the answers are 1, 3 and 6

404 One example of an extinct species is the giant elk *Megaloceros giganteus* of the last Ice Age. The last ones died out almost 8000 years ago. But not all elk species became extinct. A similar but separate species, the elk (moose) *Alces alces*, is still alive today.

405 Sometimes extinction affects a subspecies. This is a group of animals within a species that are all very similar, and slightly different from others in the species. All tigers today belong to one species, *Panthera tigris*. There were once eight subspecies of tiger. Two have become extinct in the past 100 years, the Balinese tiger and the Javan tiger.

▶ All six living subspecies of tiger differ slightly – and all are threatened with extinction.

Bengal tiger

South China tiger

Siberian tiger

Sumatran tiger

Malayan tiger

Indochinese tiger

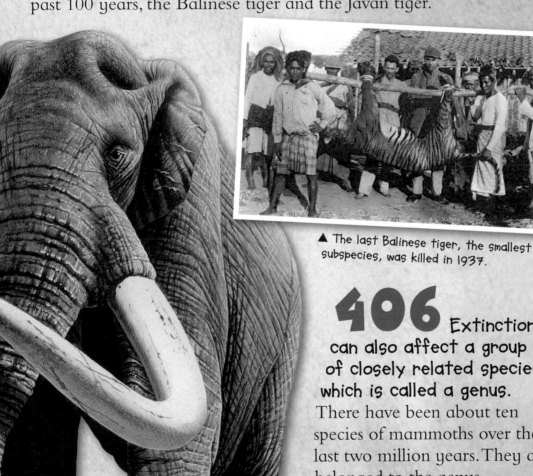

▲ The last Balinese tiger, the smallest subspecies, was killed in 1937.

406 Extinction can also affect a group of closely related species, which is called a genus. There have been about ten species of mammoths over the last two million years. They all belonged to the genus *Mammuthus*, including the woolly mammoth and the steppe mammoth. All mammoths have died out, so the genus is extinct.

◀ The Columbian mammoth, one of the biggest in the genus, died out by 12,000 years ago.

Extinction and evolution

407 Extinctions have happened through billions of years of prehistory as a natural part of evolution. Evolution is the gradual change in living things, resulting in new species appearing. As this happened, other species could not survive and became extinct.

◄ Today's hagfish differ little from their extinct cousins millions of years ago, but they are a separate species.

408 Evolution occurs as the result of changing conditions. Living things adapt to become better suited to conditions as they change, such as the weather and types of habitats (living places).

► Unlike the hagfish, the extinct armoured fish *Hemicyclaspis* from 400 million years ago has no living relatives.

I DON'T BELIEVE IT!

Trilobites were a group of marine creatures that survived for almost 300 million years. Within that time at least 18,000 kinds came and went. The last trilobites died out in a mass extinction 250 million years ago.

Trinucleus
450 million years ago

Angelina
490 million years ago

Kolihapeltis
400 million years ago

▲ Many different kinds of trilobites evolved and died out over millions of years.

409 Scientists know about long–gone extinct species from their fossils. These are remains of body parts such as the bones, teeth, horns, claws and shells of animals, and the bark, roots and leaves of plants, which have been preserved in rocks and turned to stone.

410 Studying millions of fossils of thousands of extinct species all around the world shows how different kinds of living things came and went long ago. This 'turnover' of species gives the average rate of extinction. For every one million species, one species would die out about once each year.

▲ Scientists have studied more than one million trilobite fossils.

▶ *Stegosaurus* was one of the longest-lasting dinosaur species. Its kind survived for over ten million years.

▼ Magnolias are flowering plants that have successfully evolved from 100 million years ago to today.

411 Fossil studies show the typical time for a species or genus to survive before going extinct. A mammal species lasted from one to two million years. For sea-living invertebrates (creatures without backbones) such as crabs, species survived between five and ten million years.

Why does it happen?

412 There are several reasons for extinction. Many extinctions are combinations of these reasons. We cannot know for sure why prehistoric species became extinct. But we can see the reasons for extinctions today. These may help us to understand what happened in the past.

413 One reason for extinction is competition. A species cannot get enough of its needs, such as food or living space, because other species need them too, and are better at getting them. These competing species may be newly evolved, or may have spread from afar.

414 A species can be forced to extinction by predators, parasites or diseases. Again, all of these could be new dangers as a result of evolution.

▼ In Australia, introduced farm animals such as sheep, and also wild rabbits, have been better than local species at gaining food.

▲ Australia's rock wallabies have suffered due to competition from sheep and goats.

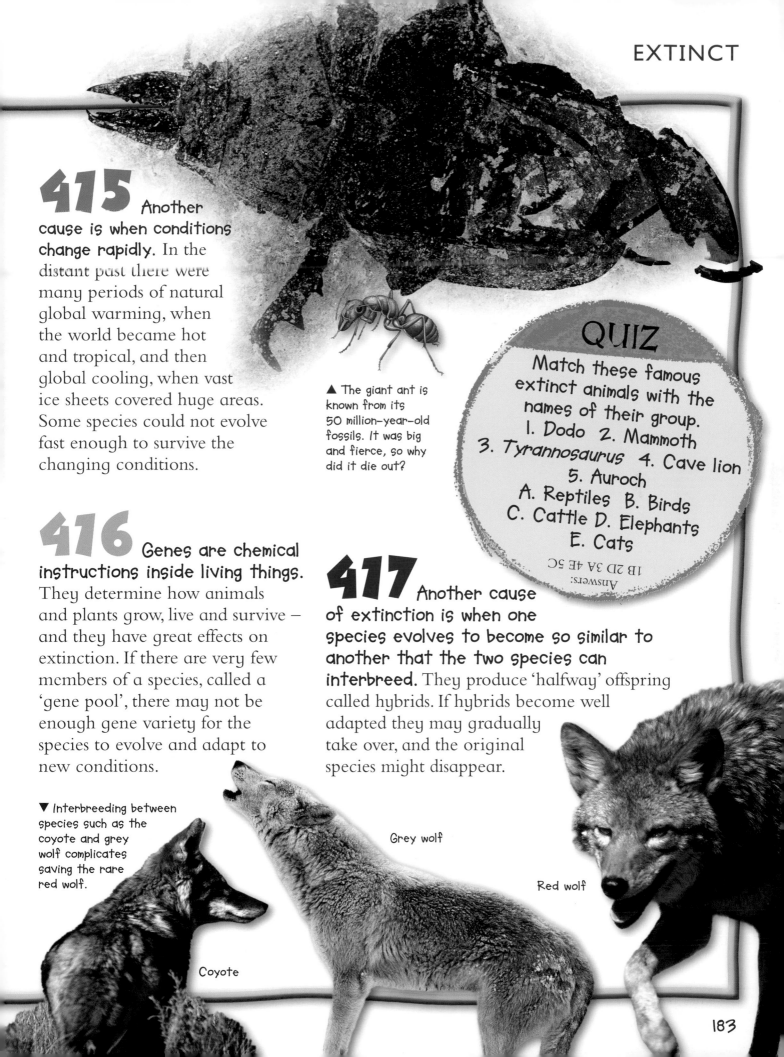

415 Another cause is when conditions change rapidly. In the distant past there were many periods of natural global warming, when the world became hot and tropical, and then global cooling, when vast ice sheets covered huge areas. Some species could not evolve fast enough to survive the changing conditions.

▲ The giant ant is known from its 50 million-year-old fossils. It was big and fierce, so why did it die out?

QUIZ

Match these famous extinct animals with the names of their group.
1. Dodo 2. Mammoth
3. Tyrannosaurus 4. Cave lion
5. Auroch
A. Reptiles B. Birds
C. Cattle D. Elephants
E. Cats

Answers:
1B 2D 3A 4E 5C

416 Genes are chemical instructions inside living things. They determine how animals and plants grow, live and survive – and they have great effects on extinction. If there are very few members of a species, called a 'gene pool', there may not be enough gene variety for the species to evolve and adapt to new conditions.

417 Another cause of extinction is when one species evolves to become so similar to another that the two species can interbreed. They produce 'halfway' offspring called hybrids. If hybrids become well adapted they may gradually take over, and the original species might disappear.

▼ Interbreeding between species such as the coyote and grey wolf complicates saving the rare red wolf.

Grey wolf

Red wolf

Coyote

183

How do we know?

418 How do we know if a species is extinct? The more recent the extinction, the harder it is to say. How long should we wait before saying a species is extinct? It might be found living in a remote area years later.

419 Wildlife experts at the IUCN (International Union for Conservation of Nature) say that a species cannot be declared extinct until 50 years have passed with no real sightings of it, or evidence such as droppings or eggshells.

▲ Leadbeater's possums were restricted to a very small area, as land around was turned into farms.

420 Sometimes, a species thought to be extinct 'comes back from the dead'. Usually it has survived in an unexplored area. It is called a 'Lazarus species' after a man in the Bible who came to life again after he died.

421 One 'Lazarus species' is the squirrel-like Leadbeater's possum of Australia. It was thought to be extinct by the 1930s, but in 1965, a group was found living in highland forests in southeast Australia. Plant 'Lazarus species' include the jellyfish tree and Monte Diablo buckwheat.

422 Some people consider creatures such as the yeti (abominable snowman), bunyip and Bigfoot to be extinct. But most scientists would say that these creatures are only from tales and legends. There is no real scientific proof they ever lived, so they cannot be extinct.

423 Some species are 'extinct in the wild'. This means all surviving members are in zoos, wildlife parks or gardens. One example is the toromiro, a tree that disappeared from Easter Island in the Pacific. Experts saved some at Kew Gardens, London, and it is now being taken back to its original home.

▶ A toromiro flower. The toromiro tree once covered parts of Easter Island, but it was wiped out in the wild.

▲ The huge, hairy yeti of the Himalayas is well known in myths and stories, but no real evidence of its existance has been discovered.

▼ In 1987, only 22 Californian condors were left in the wild. All were captured for breeding and chicks were raised using 'condor parent' puppet gloves.

FAME AT LAST

You will need:
books about Australia
the Internet

Look in books or on the Internet for information about the state of Victoria in Australia. See if you can find the state's animal emblem or symbol, and a picture of it. That's Leadbeater's possum!

Not quite extinct

◀ Pterosaurs (pterodactyls) were flying reptiles that died out with the dinosaurs 65 million years ago.

424 It's easy to decide if prehistoric species are extinct. No one has seen living dinosaurs. Some myths and legends say they exist, but there's no scientific proof. So we assume all dinosaurs are extinct.

425 Some 'Lazarus species' lived millions of years ago in prehistoric times, but have been recently rediscovered. Fossils show that the coelacanth fish died out over 60 million years ago. In 1938 one was caught off southeast Africa, with more seen since.

426 Living species (such as the coelacanth) that are very similar to long-extinct ones are known as 'living fossils'. They help us to understand how evolution works and how the original species may have become extinct.

▼ Coelacanth fish of today are not exactly the same species from millions of years ago, but very similar.

427 When a particular species is known to be living, it is called 'extant' rather than 'extinct'. Other examples of extant 'living fossils' include Australia's Wollemi pine tree, the pig-like Chacoan peccary, and the shellfish known as the lampshell.

▲ The Chacoan peccary is similar to the giant Ice Age peccary that disappeared 10,000 years ago.

428 A tree 'living fossil' once thought to be extinct is the dawn redwood. It was known only from fossils dating back ten million years. Then in 1944, examples were found in China. The living species, *Metasequoia glyptostroboides*, is slightly different to the long-extinct species.

◄ Large copper butterflies are still found in mainland Europe, but habitats lost to farming mean they are rare.

► The dawn redwood, one of only three redwood species, is now planted in parks and gardens across the world.

429 A particular plant or creature may become extinct in one area but be extant in another. In Europe the large copper butterfly became extinct in Britain in the 1860s, but it still lives in many other places across the region.

Beliefs and ideas

430 The way people view extinction has changed through the ages. Scientists' thoughts can be very different to those of other people. Some people don't believe in extinction, perhaps due to religious ideas.

431 In ancient times, people such as the Greek scientist–naturalist Aristotle (384–322 BC) believed that the natural world had never changed. No new species evolved and no old ones became extinct.

432 As people began to study fossils, they realized that they were from living things that were no longer around. Some experts said these plants and animals survived somewhere remote and undiscovered. Others began to suggest that extinction really did happen.

433 Fossil expert Georges Cuvier (1769–1832) was one of the first scientists to say that there probably were extinctions. Due to his religious beliefs, he explained them as happening in the Great Floods described in the Bible.

▼ Baron Georges Cuvier admitted that the fossil elephants he studied had become extinct.

GOOD AND BAD EXTINCTIONS

Make a list of animals that can cause problems such as spreading diseases, eating farmers' crops and damaging trees. Ask your family and friends: If you could make some extinct, which ones would you choose and why? Does everyone have the same answers? Here's a few to get you started: Houseflies, fleas, rats, squirrels, pigeons, foxes, deer.

▲ By altering the malaria-carrying mosquito's genes, scientists may be able to wipe out the disease malaria.

▼ In South America, Darwin studied fossils of the giant armadillo-like *Glyptodon* and wondered why it no longer survived.

434 **Modern views continue to change about extinction.** Scientists can now identify separate species by studying their genes, rather than what they look like or how they breed. What was thought to be one species could, with genetic information, be two or more. For endangered plants and animals, it might not be one species threatened with extinction, but several.

435 **In 1859, extinction became an important topic.** Naturalist Charles Darwin described the theory of evolution in his book *On the Origin of Species by Means of Natural Selection*. In it Darwin explained the idea of 'survival of the fittest', and how new species evolved while other species less equipped to deal with their environment died out.

▶ A scene from the 2009 movie *Creation*. Darwin's ideas about evolution shaped modern scientific views on extinction.

Long, long ago

436 The history of life on Earth dates back over three billion years, and extinction has been happening since then. Millions of plants and animals have died out over this time, called the geological timescale.

437 Fossil evidence shows that even 500 million years ago, there was an enormous variety of life with many species becoming extinct. The idea that long ago there were just a few species, which gradually increased through to today, with new ones evolving but very few dying out, is not accurate.

▼ Spiny sharks such as *Acanthodes* flourished in Devonian times but gradually died out.

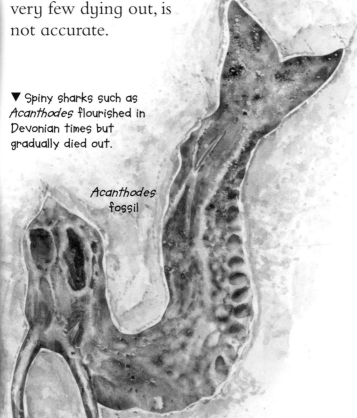

Acanthodes fossil

MILLIONS OF YEARS AGO

2.0	QUATERNARY
23	NEOGENE
	PALEOGENE
65	
	CRETACEOUS
145	
	JURASSIC
199	
	TRIASSIC
251	
	PERMIAN
299	
	CARBONIFEROUS
359	
	DEVONIAN
416	SILURIAN
443	
	ORDOVICIAN
488	
	CAMBRIAN
540	

CENOZOIC ERA

MESOZOIC ERA

PALEOZOIC ERA

PERIOD

▲ The geological timescale spans the history of the Earth. This vast amount of time is broken down into eras, and then into time periods. By studying fossils from different periods we can see how abundant life was through prehistory.

Glossopteris fossil

▲ *Glossopteris* or Gondwana tree once covered huge areas, but disappeared.

438
As we find more fossils, the gaps or 'missing links' in the history of life are filled, and we identify more and more extinctions. Fossils show how whole groups of prehistoric living things started, spread and became common, then faded away. For example, there are many kinds of reptiles alive today, such as crocodiles, snakes, lizards and turtles. But other reptiles, such as dinosaurs, pterosaurs and ichthyosaurs, are long extinct.

▼ Ichthyosaurs became extinct with the dinosaurs, 65 million years ago.

Ichthyosaur fossil

QUIZ
Match these extinct animals with their descriptions:
1. Pterosaur 2. Ichthyosaur
3. Early amphibian
A. Dolphin-shaped sea reptile
B. Four-legged swamp-dweller with a fishy tail C. Flying creature with long, thin jaws and claws on its wings and feet

Answers: 1C 2A 3B

439
Fossils also reveal that during some time periods, life was very varied, with lots of new species appearing and others dying out. At other times, plants and animals were less numerous and varied, with fewer new species evolving and lower numbers of extinctions.

▼ *Acanthostega* was one of the first four-legged land creatures.

Acanthostega fossil

◄ The extinct fish *Tiktaalik* shows a link between fish and land animals.

Tiktaalik fossil

191

Mass extinctions

440 At times in the Earth's history there have been mass extinctions, also called extinction events. Huge numbers of living things died out in a short time, usually less than a few thousand years. In some cases over half of all animals and plants disappeared.

ORDOVICIAN–SILURIAN
450–443 million years ago

Endoceras:
A type of mollusc

CAMBRIAN–ORDOVICIAN
488 million years ago

Pikaia:
An eel-like creature with a rod-like spinal column

▶ These are just a few of the millions of animals and plants that died out during mass extinctions.

441 The Cambrian–Ordovician mass extinction was 488 million years ago. It marked the change from the time span called the Cambrian Period to the next one, the Ordovician Period. Among the victims were many kinds of trilobites and lampshells, a kind of shellfish.

442 The Ordovician–Silurian mass extinction happened 450–443 million years ago, in two bursts. All life was in the sea at that time. Many types of shellfish, echinoderms (starfish, sea urchins and relatives) and corals died out.

▶ Mass extinctions show as dips in the variety of living things throughout prehistoric time.

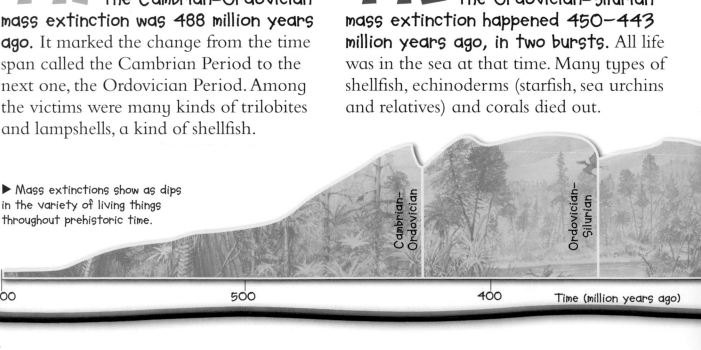

Cambrian–Ordovician

Ordovician–Silurian

600   500   400   Time (million years ago)

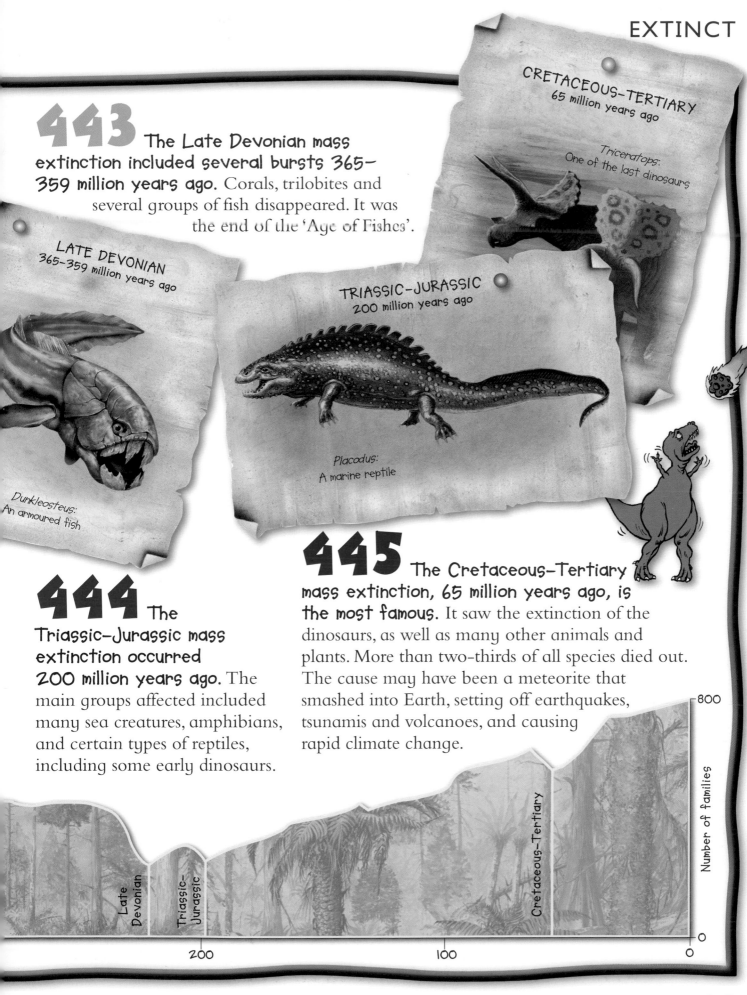

CRETACEOUS–TERTIARY
65 million years ago

Triceratops:
One of the last dinosaurs

443 The Late Devonian mass extinction included several bursts 365–359 million years ago. Corals, trilobites and several groups of fish disappeared. It was the end of the 'Age of Fishes'.

LATE DEVONIAN
365–359 million years ago

TRIASSIC–JURASSIC
200 million years ago

Placodus:
A marine reptile

Dunkleosteus:
An armoured fish

444 The Triassic–Jurassic mass extinction occurred 200 million years ago. The main groups affected included many sea creatures, amphibians, and certain types of reptiles, including some early dinosaurs.

445 The Cretaceous–Tertiary mass extinction, 65 million years ago, is the most famous. It saw the extinction of the dinosaurs, as well as many other animals and plants. More than two-thirds of all species died out. The cause may have been a meteorite that smashed into Earth, setting off earthquakes, tsunamis and volcanoes, and causing rapid climate change.

Late Devonian

Triassic–Jurassic

Cretaceous–Tertiary

Number of families

800

0

200

100

0

The biggest of all

446 The most massive of all mass extinctions was the Permian-Triassic or end-of Permian event, 251 million years ago. Also known as the 'Great Dying' it saw vast losses with more than four-fifths of all Earth's species wiped out.

447 The 'Great Dying' was probably caused by the same combination of reasons as several other mass extinctions. These included volcanic eruptions, earthquakes and tsunamis. They were probably set off by the continents drifting into new positions, with accompanying changes in sea levels, ocean currents, wind patterns, rainfall and temperature.

448 The changes that probably caused mass extinctions were very complicated because of the way species depend on each other. If a particular plant could not cope with the changes and died out, then the animals that fed on it were also affected, as were the predators that fed on them. The balance of nature was upset and extinctions followed.

▶ At the end of the Permian Period, the world was rocked by a series of great changes that killed off most kinds of life on Earth.

Acanthodian fish

Crinoids

Placoderms

449 **Mass extinctions upset some habitats more than others.** In many of these events, including the Permian-Triassic one, most losses were marine life. Especially affected were tiny sea plants and creatures that formed the floating 'soup' of life known as plankton.

Diictodon

Lystrosaurus

Gorgonops

450 **Mass extinctions were not total disasters.** Afterwards, fewer species meant less competition. So there were chances and opportunities for a surge of evolution and new species. Just 20 million years after the Permian-Triassic 'Great Dying', the first dinosaurs were prowling the land while early pterosaurs flapped through the skies.

Corals

Trilobites

Ages of ice

351 Over the past few million years there have been several extinctions linked to more than a dozen ice ages. The first of these started around 2.6 million years ago and the last one faded just 15,000–10,000 years ago. These cold times are called glaciations, and the warmer periods between – like the one today – are interglacials.

352 An example of an extinct ice age species is the sabre-tooth cat *Smilodon*. There were perhaps five species of *Smilodon* starting around 2.5 million years ago. The last one, dying out only 10,000 years ago, was *Smilodon fatalis*.

▲ Last of the ice age sabre-tooth cats, *Smilodon* lived in the Americas and was as big as the largest big cat of today, the Siberian tiger.

353 Hundreds of other ice age animals have died out in the past 25,000 years. They include the woolly rhino, woolly mammoth, cave bear, dire wolf, and various kinds of horses, deer, camels, llamas, beavers, ground sloths, and even mice and rats.

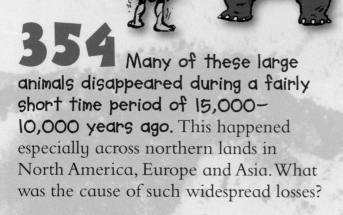

354
Many of these large animals disappeared during a fairly short time period of 15,000–10,000 years ago. This happened especially across northern lands in North America, Europe and Asia. What was the cause of such widespread losses?

356
The second reason is the spread of humans. As the climate warmed, ice sheets and glaciers melted, and people moved north into new areas. Big animals such as mammoths were hunted for food, as shown in Stone Age cave paintings. Others, such as cave bears, were killed because they were dangerous.

▼ Low sea levels during ice ages allowed people to spread from eastern Asia to North America.

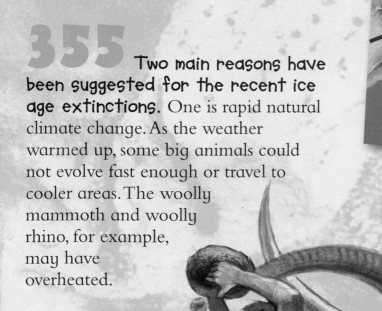

ARCTIC OCEAN

SIBERIA

NORTH AMERICA

Alaska

PACIFIC OCEAN

355
Two main reasons have been suggested for the recent ice age extinctions. One is rapid natural climate change. As the weather warmed up, some big animals could not evolve fast enough or travel to cooler areas. The woolly mammoth and woolly rhino, for example, may have overheated.

▶ Stone Age people probably trapped and killed mammoths, which would have provided them with food for weeks.

Keeping a record

457 In ancient times, people travelled little and did not record details of nature, so extinctions were hard to identify. From the 1500s, people began to explore the world, study living things and discover new species. They then hunted, shot, ate or collected them – some to extinction.

▲ People exploring remote areas brought back tales of fanciful beasts – perhaps the result of several real creatures that explorers mixed up.

459 All elephant birds were extinct by the 1500s. People not only hunted them, but also collected and cooked their huge eggs, more than 35 centimetres in length.

458 Spectacular examples of historical extinction are the elephant birds of Madagascar. There were several species of these giant, flightless birds, similar to ostriches but larger. The biggest stood 3 metres tall and weighed more than 450 kilograms.

▼ Elephant birds evolved on the island of Madagascar with no big predators to threaten them – until humans arrived.

Steller's sea cow was 8 metres long

▲ Extinctions of large creatures continued through recent centuries.

Bluebuck lived in small herds

Great auks once numbered millions

460 There is a long list of other animal species that went extinct even before 1900. They include the tall New Zealand ground birds called moas (by 1500), the huge European cow known as the auroch (probably 1630s), the North Pacific Steller's sea cow (1760s), the Southern African bluebuck antelope (around 1800) and the Atlantic penguin-like great auk (1850s).

I DON'T BELIEVE IT!

The huge moa of New Zealand was 4 metres tall. It was hunted by the enormous Haast's eagle, the biggest known eagle, which became extinct by 1400.

461 Many plants are also recorded as going extinct during this time. They include the Rio myrtle tree from South America (about 1820s), the string tree from the Atlantic island of St Helena (1860s) and the Indian kerala tree (1880s).

◄ St Helena ebony is a shrub that is being rescued from the brink of extinction.

Gathering pace

462 Over the last 100 years, the rate of extinction has speeded up greatly. More kinds of living things are disappearing than ever before. This is due mainly to human activity such as cutting down forests, habitat loss as natural areas are changed for farmland and houses, hunting, collecting rare species, and releasing chemicals into the environment.

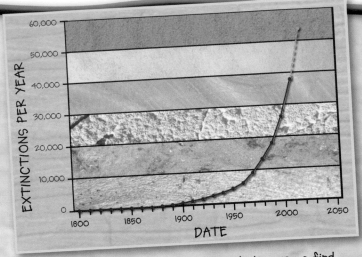

▲ The estimated extinction rate is rocketing as we find out about more threatened species every year.

▶ The spectacled bear of South America's Andes Mountains faces many threats, including the logging of its forest home.

463 One of the first extinctions to receive lots of publicity around the world was the Caribbean monk seal in the 1950s. It was hunted for its oil and meat, and to stop it eating the fish that people wanted to catch. From 2003, expeditions tried to find it again but gave up after five years.

▼ The last confirmed sightings of Caribbean monk seals were southeast of the island of Jamaica in 1952.

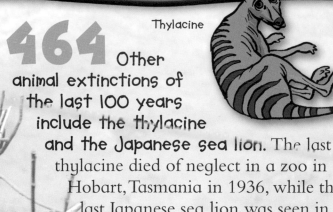

Thylacine

464 Other animal extinctions of the last 100 years include the thylacine and the Japanese sea lion. The last thylacine died of neglect in a zoo in Hobart, Tasmania in 1936, while the last Japanese sea lion was seen in 1974. Many plant species have also died out in the last 100 years, including the Cuban holly (1950s), the cry violet or cry pansy in France (1950s) and the woolly begonia of Malaysia (1960s).

465 With each passing year scientists explore, identify and record more living species in more detail than ever before. As we study and list all of these new plants and animals, we have a greater chance of discovering when one goes extinct.

▼ The Bosavi silky cuscus is a rarity – a new species discovered in Papua New Guinea.

FIND THAT SEAL!

You will need:
paper   pens

Imagine you are on an expedition to search for the Caribbean monk seal. Make a list of the equipment you would need. Binoculars, cameras, sketch pad, sound recorder… You need evidence, so don't forget specimen bottles for some of the seal's hair, or its urine or droppings!

Too many to disappear

466 The passenger pigeon was once extremely common. Flocks of millions flew around North America, darkening the skies as they passed. Before Europeans arrived in North America, native people caught the pigeons for their meat and feathers. This was on a small scale and happened for centuries without affecting the overall number of birds.

467 With the arrival of Europeans, especially from about 1700, came many changes. The new settlers altered the land from natural habitats to farms, roads and towns. Habitat loss soon gathered pace, and people also began to catch the pigeons for a cheap supply of food.

▼ Today, birds such as these city starlings seem too numerous to vanish. But we cannot be sure how they will fare in the future.

▶ Passenger pigeons became big business, with hunters shooting and trappers netting the birds to sell their meat in cities.

▲ Famous hunter, naturalist and artist John James Audobon painted passenger pigeons. He once said one flock was 'still passing in undiminished numbers... for three days'.

468 By the 1850s, the hunters and trappers noticed that passenger pigeon numbers had started to fall. But the killing continued. Some people tried to raise the pigeons in captivity, but the birds could only breed and thrive in very large flocks. Kept in small groups, they did not eat well or breed. They may have also suffered from a bird illness called Newcastle disease.

469 By 1900, the passenger pigeon had just about disappeared in the wild. The last one in captivity, Martha, died in Cincinnati Zoo, Ohio, USA in 1914. With her went one of the most numerous birds that ever existed.

I DON'T BELIEVE IT!

Martha, the last passenger pigeon, was named after Martha Washington, wife of the first US president George Washington. There are several statues and memorials to Martha (the pigeon), including one at Cincinnati Zoo.

▲ Passenger pigeons did not survive well in captivity. When the last one died in 1914, it was mounted or 'stuffed' at the Smithsonian Institute.

203

Island extinctions

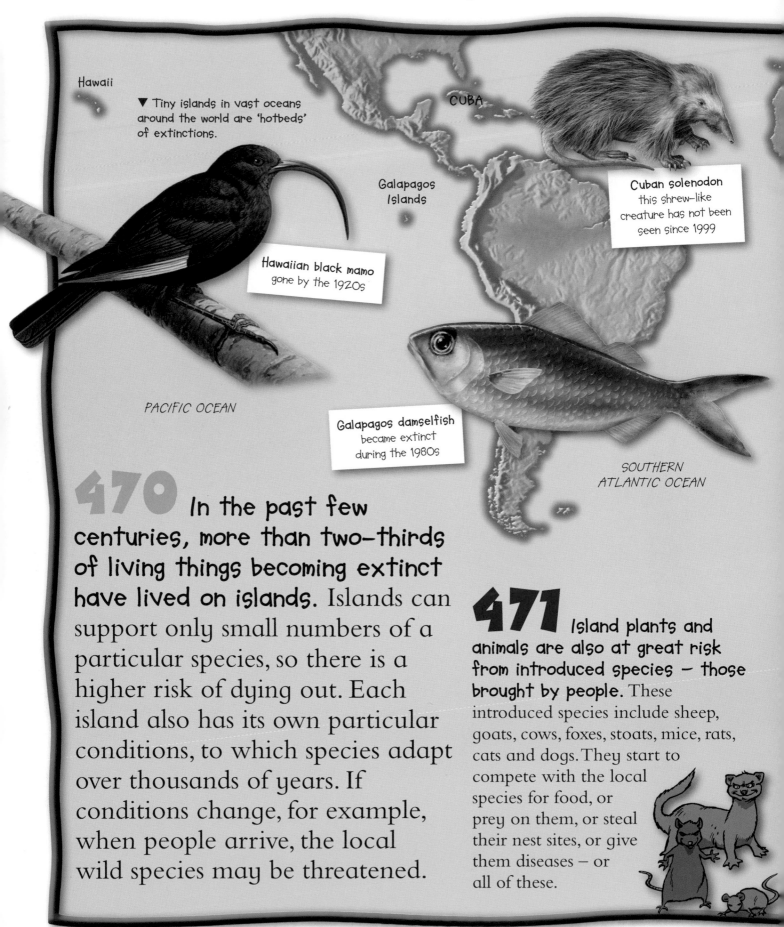

▼ Tiny islands in vast oceans around the world are 'hotbeds' of extinctions.

Hawaii

CUBA

Galapagos Islands

Cuban solenodon this shrew-like creature has not been seen since 1999

Hawaiian black mamo gone by the 1920s

PACIFIC OCEAN

Galapagos damselfish became extinct during the 1980s

SOUTHERN ATLANTIC OCEAN

470 In the past few centuries, more than two-thirds of living things becoming extinct have lived on islands. Islands can support only small numbers of a particular species, so there is a higher risk of dying out. Each island also has its own particular conditions, to which species adapt over thousands of years. If conditions change, for example, when people arrive, the local wild species may be threatened.

471 Island plants and animals are also at great risk from introduced species – those brought by people. These introduced species include sheep, goats, cows, foxes, stoats, mice, rats, cats and dogs. They start to compete with the local species for food, or prey on them, or steal their nest sites, or give them diseases – or all of these.

PACIFIC OCEAN

MAURITIUS

Lesser bilby
not seen on the island
continent of Australia
since the 1950s

AUSTRALIA

INDIAN OCEAN

Mauritius dodo
disappeared by
the 1690s

THE DODO LIVES AGAIN!

You will need:
sheet of card   scissors   coloured pens
sticky tape   elastic

Cut out a face mask in the shape of a dodo's head and beak and colour it as shown (left). Find out from books or the Internet about the noises a dodo made. Now you can try to bring the dodo back to life!

472 Perhaps the most famous example of any extinct animal is the dodo. This flightless, turkey-sized bird lived on Mauritius in the Indian Ocean, ate fruit and nested on the ground. It had no natural predators or enemies. Then people arrived with animals that hunted it, its eggs and its chicks. By 1700, the dodo was gone, leading to the saying 'dead as a dodo'.

473 At least 50 bird species from the Hawaiian Islands are extinct. This affected other wildlife. Some of the birds fed on nectar and carried pollen so that flowers could breed. Others ate fruits and spread the seeds in their droppings. Without the birds, some of these plants become extinct. When one species disappears, then another that depends on it dies out, it is known as co-extinction.

What's happening today?

474 In the natural world today, extinction rates are shooting up due to a huge variety of causes. Scientists call this another time of mass extinction.

475 The main cause of today's extinctions is habitat loss and degradation (changing natural habitats for the worse). The number of people in the world is rising fast and they need land for their houses, farms, factories, roads and leisure, leaving less wild areas.

▲ Acid rain from polluting gases taken up by clouds has devastated large areas of forest.

◀ Logging and other forms of deforestation are major threats in tropical areas.

476 Other causes include pollution and hunting for food or trophies. There is also the collecting of species for displays, introduced species, and diseases that spread from domestic animals and farm plants to wild species. As the early signs of global warming and climate change become more marked, these will also have huge effects on habitats and push species towards extinction.

▲ The baiji is probably now extinct. Some people hope it survives in backwaters of the Yangtze and nearby rivers. There are rare sightings, but for the time being, no proof.

477 In 2007, a search in China failed to find any baijis, or Yangtze river dolphins. This species was threatened for many reasons, including dams built across its rivers, pollution, hunting and the overfishing of its natural prey.

▼ Now extinct, golden toads were probably victims of global warming and increased human activity in their natural habitats.

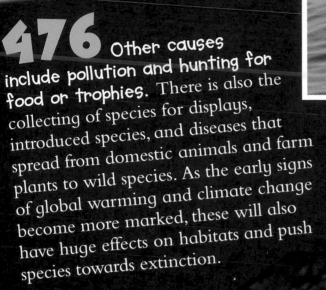

On the brink

478 Every year, wildlife experts make lists of animals and plants that are threatened with extinction. These are known as the IUCN 'Red Lists', and every year, they grow longer.

▶ Symbols indicate if a species is threatened or not, ranging from LC meaning Least Concern, to EX meaning Extinct.

QUIZ

Which of these amphibians is threatened with extinction?
1. Lungless Mexican salamander
2. South African ghost frog
3. Betic midwife toad
4. Chinese giant salamander
5. Darwin frog

Answer:
All of them, plus thousands of others

479 One of the most endangered groups of animals is the rhinos. There are only five rhino species and all are in huge trouble. The black, Javan and Sumatran rhinos are listed as 'critically endangered'. They will become extinct in 20–50 years unless massive efforts are made to save them.

White rhino

▼ All rhinos need action to save them. Most numerous is the white rhino, with less than 20,000.

Javan rhino

Sumatran rhino

Black rhino

480 A larger group, with many species at risk of extinction, is the amphibians. More than half of the 6000-plus species are threatened. A terrible problem is the new fungus infection called chytrid disease. Recent amphibian extinctions include the gastric-brooding frog of Australia, which swallowed its eggs so the tadpoles could grow in its stomach. It died out in the 1980s.

▲ Baby gastric-brooding frogs emerged from their mother's mouth. Many other species of frogs, toads and newts are also under threat.

▲ The world's largest flower, rafflesia, is now extremely rare.

481 You cannot get closer to extinction than only one remaining individual. The café marron bush grew on the island of Rodrigues in the Indian Ocean, but finally only one bush was left. Scientists at Kew Gardens, London took cuttings from it in the 1980s and grew them into bushes. Now some are being taken back to Rodrigues.

Indian rhino

482 Coral reefs are among the world's richest places for wildlife. But these whole habitats may become extinct in the next 100–200 years. They are in great danger from threats such as global warming, pollution, water cloudiness and acidity upsetting the delicate natural balance between their species.

▶ Due to global warming, coral reefs may become 'bleached' and die.

Saved just in time

483 To save an almost extinct species takes time, effort and money. This means studying it and its habitat, its contact with other species and finding out how many are left. Scientists assess its needs through field studies – in the wild – and also captive studies. They establish what it eats, where it nests or which soil it likes, so that places can be put aside.

▲ Through a huge conservation effort, the numbers of ladybird spiders in Great Britain have risen.

Female

Male

484 Rescuing a threatened animal or plant from extinction also means saving its habitat. Without somewhere natural and safe to live, the species cannot thrive in the wild. Otherwise, even if it is saved, it will always be limited to a park, zoo or similar place, and be extinct in the wild.

▼ In North America, movements of very rare black-footed ferrets are studied by radio transmitter collars.

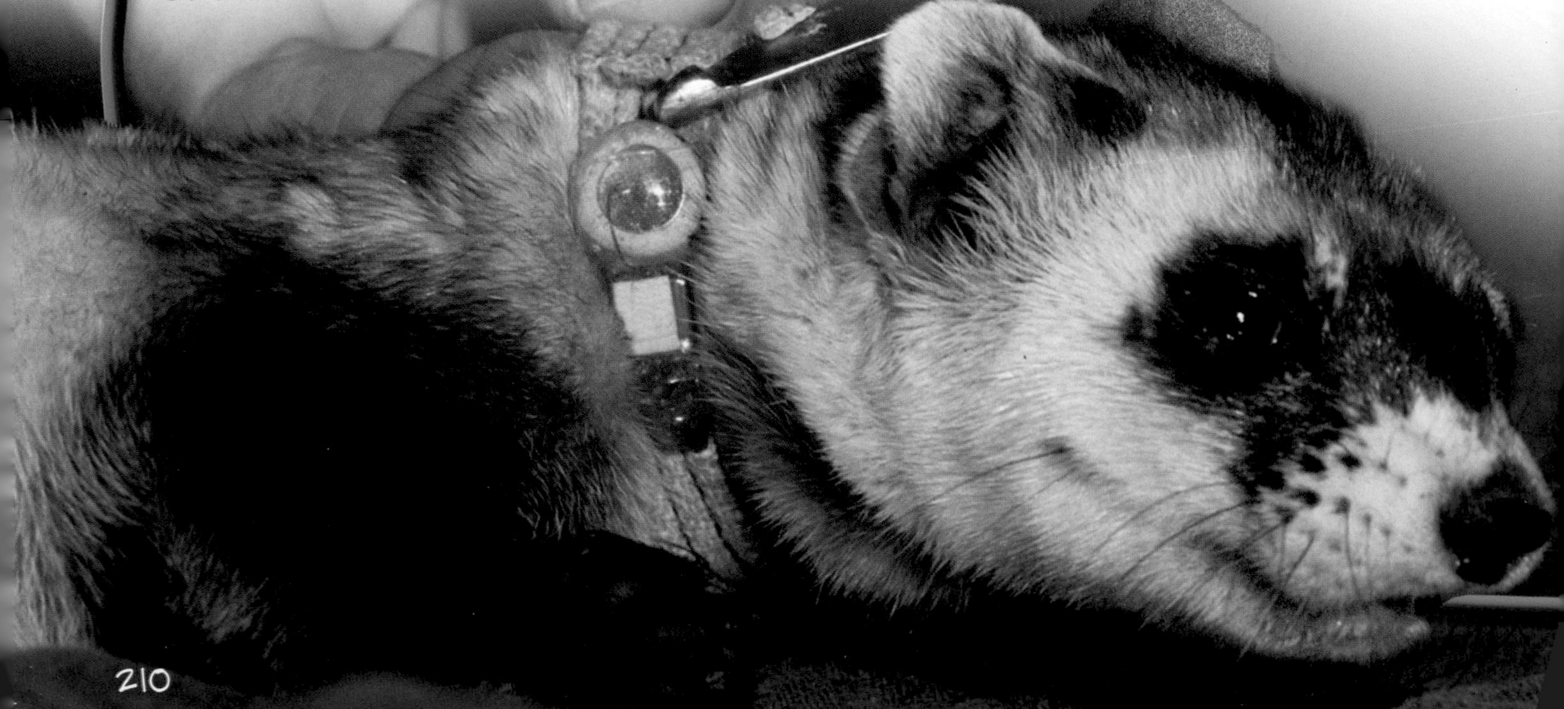

You will need:
large sheet of paper
coloured pens

Spiders may not be everyone's favourite animal, but they deserve saving as much as other species. Find out about the ladybird spider, which is almost extinct in Britain. Make a colourful poster telling people why it should not be allowed to die out.

485 It's less use people coming to an area from far away, and trying to save a species, than local people getting involved. The locals need to have input into the rescue effort. Through ecotourism, visitors can see rare wildlife without damaging it or the habitat and pay money, which is put towards conservation efforts.

◀ Elephant safaris allow paying tourists to get close to rare rhinos without disturbing them too much.

486 Saving one 'flagship' or 'headline' species from extinction can help to save whole habitats. Such species usually appeal to the public because they are big and powerful, like tigers and mountain gorillas, or cute and fluffy, like giant pandas and golden lion tamarins.

▼ Setting up wildlife parks and nature reserves helps not only the headline species, such as these gorillas, but all the plants and animals living there.

Should we care?

487 **Why should we care if a species goes extinct?** Especially if it is some small bug in a remote forest, or a worm on the seabed. Does it really matter or affect us in any way?

488 **Many people think that all animals and plants have a right to be here on Earth.** We should not destroy nature for little reason. If we let species die out, it shows we do not care for our surroundings and the natural world. These types of reasons are known as moral and ethical arguments.

489 **There are medical reasons for saving species.** Researchers may discover that a particular type of plant or animal is the source of a new wonder drug to cure illness. If it had gone extinct, we would never know this. Other species can be used for medical research into diseases such as cancers.

490 **Scientific reasons to prevent species dying out are also important.** Extinction reduces biodiversity, which is the variety of living things necessary for the balance of nature. The genes in certain animals or plants could be used in GM, genetic modification, perhaps to improve our farm crops and make our farm animals healthier.

491 **There are also traditional and cultural reasons for caring about extinction.** Some endangered species are important to ethnic groups and tribes for their history, ceremonies, myths and special foods. People should not come to an area from afar with new ways of living and cause habitat loss, introduce new animals, plants and diseases and kill off local species.

▲ The Florida panther is an extremely rare subspecies of cougar, or mountain lion. If it dies out, there will still be other cougars elsewhere. So would its disappearance matter?

I DON'T BELIEVE IT!

In the 1800s, European explorers in Australia captured now-extinct creatures including pig-footed bandicoots. But when the explorers got lost and hungry, they ate the bandicoots.

Gone forever?

492 People once thought that extinction is forever, but future science may change this view. The idea of bringing extinct animals or plants back to life can be seen through films such as *Jurassic Park*. Scientists use a species' eggs, its genes or its genetic material such as DNA (de-oxyribonucleic acid).

▲ In the *Jurassic Park* stories, dinosaurs were recreated from their preserved genes and hatched in egg incubators.

▼ Why the Pyrenean ibex died out is unclear, but it may have been the result of infectious diseases.

493 In 2009, a baby Pyrenean ibex, a subspecies of the goat-like Spanish ibex, was born. Its mother was a goat but its genes came from one of the last Pyrenean ibexes, which had died out by 2000. The young ibex was a genetic copy. It died after birth, but it showed what might be possible in future.

QUIZ

Put these species in order of when they became extinct, from longest ago to most recent.
1. Quagga
2. Dodo
3. Neanderthal humans
4. Baiji (Yangtze river dolphin)
5. Woolly mammoth

Answers:
3. About 30,000 years ago
5. Around 10,000 years ago
2. By 1700 1. 1883 4. By 2007 (probably)

494 To revive extinct species, there are many problems to solve in genetic engineering, altering DNA, cloning and similar methods. However scientists are taking samples of DNA and other material from all kinds of sources, such as frozen mammoths, dodo bones, the dead seeds of extinct plants, and even long-gone humans, to carry out experiments and see what can be done.

▲ The Barbary lion of North Africa was thought to be extinct from the 1920s, but genetic tests have revealed several living in zoos.

▼ The Quagga Project selects and breeds the most quagga–like zebras over many generations.

495 The quagga, which went extinct in 1883, was a subspecies of the plains zebra of southern Africa. It had zebra stripes on its front half but was plain brown at the rear. The Quagga Project aims to 'breed back' quaggas. This is done by choosing plains zebras that look most like quaggas, and allowing them to mate. Gradually, after several generations, the young of plains zebras should look more and more like quaggas.

215

Looking to the future

496 In the future, living things will continue to go extinct, with or without human meddling — because that is the nature of life and how it evolves. The damage we are doing to the world, especially with habitat loss and climate change, means that the rate of extinction will only increase.

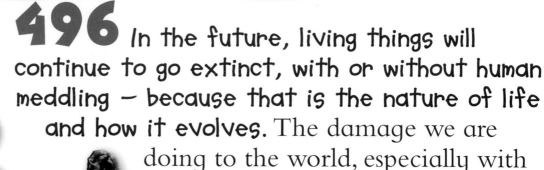

Ardipithecus ramidus
Extinct: 4.5 million years ago

Australopithecus afarensis
Extinct: 3.5 million years ago

Homo ergaster
Extinct: 1.9 million years ago

Homo erectus
Extinct: 1.7 million years ago

497 What about our own kind, human beings? Over the past four million years there have probably been more than 20 different species of humans and their close cousins on Earth. Only one is left now – ourselves, modern humans, known as *Homo sapiens*. All others have gone extinct.

▲ There have been many different species of human throughout history. Despite advances such as stone tools and controlling fire, they all became extinct.

498 A recent human extinction is the Neanderthal people, *Homo neanderthalensis*. They lived about 250,000 years ago across northern Europe and Asia. As modern humans spread from Africa into Europe and Asia, Neanderthals died out. Whether modern people killed them, or were better at finding food and shelter, is not clear.

I DON'T BELIEVE IT!
Recent surveys indicate that 1 in 8 bird species are at risk of extinction, and within 100 years this could rise to 1 in 4. And birds are a lot less threatened than many other animal groups.

499 Surviving even later than the Neanderthals, but still becoming extinct, were the 'hobbit people' on the island of Flores, Southeast Asia. Known as *Homo floresiensis*, they were only about one metre tall. They may have survived until less than 15,000 years ago.

▶ The remains of *Homo floresiensis* were discovered in 2003. It may be a new species of extinct human.

Homo floresiensis
Extinct: 15,000 years ago

Homo heidelbergensis
Extinct: 600,000 years ago

Homo neanderthalensis
Extinct: 100,000 years ago

500 In the distant future, will humans become extinct? Our knowledge of the natural world, and the harm we are doing it, suggests that our species will not last forever. But humans have shown great skill at surviving all kinds of problems, and are likely to carry on for a very long time yet.

▶ Can modern humans use their wit and intelligence to survive – whilst also saving wild species?

Homo sapiens
Still alive today

INDEX

Page numbers in **bold** refer to main entries; page numbers in *italics* refer to illustrations.

A

absolute dating 154
Acanthodes 190
Acanthostega 16, 16, 33, 191
acid rain *206*
Africa *see* North Africa; South Africa
Age of Dinosaurs 52–53, 59
Albertosaurus 94, 115, 116, **117**
Alectrosaurus 115, 116
alligators 82
Allodesmus 41
Allosaurus 52, 66, 67, *89, 95,* 115
Alxasaurus 65
amber 33, *33,* 146, *146*
ammonites 13, *13,* 138, *138, 144, 144,* 150, *150,* 152, 153, 171, *171*
ammonoid *70–71*
amphibians 16, 17, 18, 20, 33, 209
Anancus 36, 37
anatomy, *T rex* **98–99,** 122
Andrewsarchus 31, 31, 82–83, 97
ankylosaur 75, 168, *168*
Anning, Mary 156, *156*
Anomalocaris 10–11, 11
Antarctica 90
ants *183*
Apatosaurus 61, 61, 65, *65*
apes 46, 47
Aphaneramma 17
Appalachiosaurus 115, 117
Archaeopteryx 25, 25, 33, 33, 91, 121, 159, 173, *173*
Archelon 70–71
archosaurs 55
Ardipithecus 47
Argentavis 42, 42
Argentina 90

Argentinosaurus 62
Aristotle 188
armadillos 45
armoured dinosaurs **74–75**
armoured fish 14, *14, 180*
arms, *T rex* 99, **104,** *104, 112,* 117
Arsinoitherium 31, 31, 82–83
Arthropleura 16, 16–17
arthropods 12, 16
Asia *see* Central Asia; East Asia
asteroid impact 81
aurochs *9,* 49, *199*
Australia *182*
Australopithecus afarensis 48, *48*
Austroraptor 51
Aviatyrannis 112
Avimimus 94

B

babies, dinosaur 77, **78–79, 110**
baiji 207, *207*
Barbary lion *215*
Barosaurus 52, 52, 62
Baryonyx 61, 61, 65
bats 137, *137,* 159
beaks 61
Beipiaosaurus 65
belemnites 139, *139*
belemnoid *70–71*
Bible 138
birds 13, 25, 33, 42, 71, 91, 121, 139, 168, 173, *173*
bite strength 103, 106, 109
black-footed ferret *210*
blue-green algae 154
bluebuck antelope 199, *199*
bone-head dinosaurs (pachycephalosaurs) 84
bones 136, 137, *137,* 142, 162, 168, *168*
Bosavi silky cuscus *201*
Brachiosaurus 62, 63, 63, 76, 95, *96*
brains, dinosaur 84, 101, *101*

Branchiosaurus 20
Branisella 82–83
brontosaur trackways *62*
Brontotherium 30, *30*
Brown, Barnum 118, 119, *119*
Burgess Shale 149, *149*
butterflies 187, *187*

C

café marron bush 209
Cambrian Period 149, 150, 151
camels 39
Carboniferous Period 151
Carboniferous swamp *176–177*
Carcharodontosaurus 66, 66–67, 129, *129*
Caribbean monk seal 200, *200*
carnivores (meat-eaters) 52, 53, **66–67,** 94, 97, *98,* 115, *121,* 128
cast fossils *144,* **144–145,** 145
Caudipteryx 91
causes of extinction **182–183,** 194, 206–207
cave bear 41, *41,* 196, 197
cave lion 8, *8,* 9
cave-people 85
Cenozoic Era 53
Central Asia 76, 90
ceratopsians (horn-face dinosaurs) 75
Chacoan peccary 187, *187*
Charnia 11, *11*
Chasmatosaurus 23, 23
chimpanzees 47
China 79, 85, 90, 91
Chriacus 82–83
claws, dinosaur **64–65**
climate change 197, 207, 209
Climatius 14, *14*
cloning 214–215
coelacanth fish 172, *172,* 186, *186,* 187
Coelophysis 73, 73
cold-blooded animals 121

G

Galapagos damselfish *204*
Gallimimus 61, *61*
Gastornis 82–83
gastric-brooding frogs 209, *209*
genes 189, 213, 214–215
genus 179
geological timescale **150–151**, 190, *190*
Gerrothorax 16
giant ant *183*
giant elk (*Megaloceros giganteus*) 178, *178*
giant sloth 45
Giganotosaurus 66, *66–67*, 128
Gigantopithecus 46, 47, *47*
glaciations **196–197**
global warming 183, 207, 209
Glyptodon 45, *45*, *189*
Gobi Desert 76
golden toads *207*
Gondwana tree *191*
Gorgosaurus 115, **116**, *116*
gorillas *211*
Grand Canyon, USA 152, *152*
graptolites 151, *151*, 153
great auks 199, *199*
'Great Dying' 194
grey wolf 183
growing up, *T rex* **110**
Gryphea 138, *138*
Guanlong 114, *114*

H

habitat loss 200, 206
hadrosaurs *78–79*, *94*, 106
hagfish *180*
Hatcher, John Bell 118
hatchlings 78, *78–79*
Hawaiian black mamo *204*
head crests 69
head-to-head butting 84, *84*

Hemicyclaspis 14
Hendrickson, Sue 124, *124*
herbivores (plant-eaters) 52, 53, 59, 74, *94*, 95, 96, *98*, 106
herds 62, 107
Herrerasaurus 56, *56*, 95
Hesperocyon 40, *40*
Hesperornis 70–71
Homo erectus 48, *48–49*
horn-face dinosaurs (ceratopsians) 75
horns 39, *39*, 74, *74*, 75
horses 28, 29, 38, 42, 44
humans 32, 41, *41*, 46, 47, **48–47**, 53, 147, *147*, 173, **216–217**, *216–217*
hunting 95, 106, **108**, 128, 197, *197*, 200, 207
hybrids 183
Hylaeosaurus 90
Hylonomus 19, *19*
Hypsilophodon 64
Hyracotherium 38, *38*, *82–83*, 150, *150*

I

ice 147, *147*
ice ages **8–7**, 36, 41, **196–197**
Ichthyornis 71, *71*
ichthyosaurs 70, 142, *142*, 156, *191*
Ichthyosaurus 70–71
Ichthyostega 17, *17*
Iguanodon 65, 73, 85, 90, 141
index fossils 153, *153*
insects 11, 12, 16, 33, 82
intelligence, dinosaur 84, 101
interbreeding 183, *183*
introduced species 204, 207
island extinctions **204–205**

J

'Jane' 127, *127*
jawless fish 14

jellyfish 11, 148, 149, *149*, 159
Jurassic Period 53, 67, *95*, 112, *151*

K

kerala tree 199
keratin 64
'Kid Rex' 126
Kronosaurus 70–71

L

ladybird spiders *210*
Lagosuchus 55
Lakes, Arthur 118
Lambeosaurus *94*
lampshells 187, 192
Lazarus species 184, 186
Leadbeater's possum 184, *184*
Leaellynasaura 68, *68–69*
legs, dinosaur *54*, 56, 98, **105**, 123
Lepidodendron 151, *151*
Leptictidium 28, *28*
Lessemsaurus 57, *57*
lesser bilby *205*
'living fossils' 172, 186, 187
lizards 82
lobefin fish 15, 17
logging *206*
'Lucy' 173
Lystrosaurus 21, *21*, *52*

M

macaws *91*
Macrauchenia 44, *44*
magnetism 153, *153*
magnolias *181*
Maiasaura 78, *78–79*
males **111**
Mamenchisaurus 62
mammals 13, 25, **28–29**, 31, **34–33**, **38–37**, 41, 82, 83, 97, 121

W

X

Y

ACKNOWLEDGEMENTS

The publishers would like to thank the following sources for the use of their photographs:
t = top, b = bottom, l = left, r = right, c = centre, bg = background, m = main

Cover: *Front* (t) Roger Harris/Science Photo Library, (b) DM7/Shutterstock.com; *Spine* leonello calvetti/Shutterstock.com; *Back* (l) leonello calvetti/Shutterstock.com, (c) Michael Rosskothen/Shutterstock.com, (r) Steffen Foerster/iStockphoto.com, (b) AlienCat/Fotolia.com

Alamy 73(t) petpics; 92 Photos 12; 155 sciencephotos; 187(br) John Glover; 188 Mary Evans Picture Library; 211(c) Picture Press; 214(t) Photos 12

Burpee Museum of Natural History 127

Corbis 56(t) Louie Psihoyos; 60 Layne Kennedy; 62(cl) Louie Psihoyos; 63 Sciepro/Science Photo Library; 73(b) Walter Myers; 77(t) Handout/Reuters; 86(b) Louie Psihoyos; 87(cr) Louie Psihoyos; 102(b); 118 Bettman; 119 Bettman; 121 Layne Kennedy; 122 DK Limited; 126 Louie Psihoyos; 128 Louie Psihoyos; 134 Annie Griffiths Belt; 136 Layne Kennedy; 137 DK Limited; 146 Michael Amendolia; 159 Mike Nelson; 160 Martin Schutt; 161(t) Paul A. Souders; 162 Ted Soqui; 163(t) Reuters; 164 Michael S. Yamashita; 166 Bill Varie; 170 Ladislav Janicek/Zefa; 171(t) Louie Psihoyos; 173(c) Bettmann; 174(b) Louie Psihoyos; 183(t) Jonathan Blair; 185(br); 207(t) Alex Hofford; 207(b) Patricia Fogden; 211(b) Martin Harvey

Dreamstime.com 179(tr) South China tiger Trix1428; 202(c) Photoinjection; 209(b) Naluphoto

F.H. Idzerda 179(c)

FLPA 156 Martin B Withers

Fotolia.com 5(t) Tommy Schultz; 6(cr) Lagui; 10(t) Deborah Benbrook; 13(tr) Michael Siller; 24 EcoView; 29(tr) Vladimir Ovchinnikov; 33(br) Vatikaki; 42(tr) Ian Scott, (l) Maribell; 49(b) Magnum; 63 Vladimir Ovchinnikov; 67(tr) khz; 71(t) Peter Schinck; 75(tl) cbpix; 98(c) Tommy Schultz; 99 Desertdiver; 100–101 cornelius; 120(t) zebra0209; 137 Alexey Khromushin; 179(cr) Sumatran tiger Vladimir Wrangel; 179(br) Malayan tiger Kitch Bain; 179(br) Indochinese tiger Judy Whitton; 182(bl) clearviewstock; 187(c); 206(t) sisu; 209(c) Jefery

Getty Images 131(t) Handout; 198(b) National Geographic; 215(t) AFP

Glow Images 79(b) O. Louis Mazzatenta; 88(tl) Lynn Johnson/National Geographic Image Collection; 88(tr) Lynn Johnson/National Geographic Image Collection 89(l) Lynn Johnson/National Geographic Image Collection

iStockphoto.com 13(tl) shayes17; 36(tr) nealec; 41(bl) egdigital; 43(br) igs942; 59(t) Jouke van der Meer; 60(b) Dave Bluck; 61(tl) Anders Nygren; 69(bl) TSWinner; 71 Allister Clark; 81(br) Olga Khoroshunova; 98(b) tswinner; 98–99 MiguelAngeloSilva; 120(b) sethakan; 137(c) Håkan Karlsson

naturepl.com 200–201 Eric Baccega; 210 Andrew Harrington

NHPA 201(b) Bruce Beehler

photolibrary.com 102(t) Robert Clark; 112 Salvatore Vasapolli; 125 Steve Vider; 182(c) Paul Nevin; 183(br) Stouffer Productions; 199 Howard Rice; 212–213 Purestock

Photoshot 209(t) NHPA

Reuters 124 Ho Old; 139(t)

Rex Features 130 20thC.Fox/Everett; 132 Nils Jorgensen; 171(b) Sipa Press; 189 Icon/Everett

Royal Botanic Gardens, Kew 185(cl)

Science Photo Library 45 Jaime Chirinos; 50–51 Jose Antonio Penas; 62–63 Julius T Csotony; 65 Jose Antonio Penas; 70–71 Christian Jegou Publiphoto Diffusion; 77(b) Christian Darkin; 80–81 Steve Munsinger; 82–83 Christian Jegou; 90(t) Natural History Museum, London; 123 Volker Steger; 139(b) Sinclair Stammers; 149 Alan Sirulnikoff; 153(t) Jaroslaw Grudzinski; 157 Sheila Terry;
161(b) NASA/GSFC/METI/ERSDAC/JAROS; 165(t) Mauro Fermariello; 174(t) Pascal Goetgheluck; 176–177 Richard Bizley; 192(tr) Laurie O'Keefe; 215(b) Philippe Psaila

Shutterstock.com 1 Linda Bucklin; 5(cr) Linda Bucklin; 52–53 Eric Broder Van Dyke; 53(t) Catmando; 54(b) leonello calvetti; 56–57 George Burba; 61(b) Catmando; 64 Michael Rosskothen; 65 Marilyn Volan; 66(t) Kostyantyn Ivanyshen; 66(c) Linda Bucklin; 67(bl) DM7; 67(br) Jean-Michel Girard; 74 leonello calvetti; 75(c) Ozja; 75(b) Ralf Juergen Kraft; 91 SmudgeChris

The Kobal Collection 85(b) Moonlighting Films

TopFoto 131(b) Topham Picture Point; 198(t) Artmedia/HIP; 202(b) The Granger Collection; 203(t) The Granger Collection; 203(b) Topham Picturepoint

All other photographs are from: digitalSTOCK, digitalvision, Dreamstime.com, Fotolia.com, ImageState, iStockphoto.com, John Foxx, PhotoAlto, PhotoDisc, PhotoEssentials, PhotoPro, Stockbyte

All artworks from the Miles Kelly Artwork Bank

Every effort has been made to acknowledge the source and copyright holder of each picture.
Miles Kelly Publishing apologises for any unintentional errors or omissions.